# LIVING WITH WHAT YOU LOVE

# LIVING WITH WHAT YOU LOVE

## CREATING INTIMATE SPACES WITH FAMILY PHOTOS, CHERISHED HEIRLOOMS, AND COLLECTIBLES

### MONICA RICH KOSANN

FOREWORD BY ALEXA HAMPTON
PHOTOGRAPHS BY STEVEN RANDAZZO

CLARKSON
POTTER/
PUBLISHERS
NEW YORK

# FOR MY FAMILY

ALL RIGHTS RESERVED.
PUBLISHED IN THE UNITED STATES BY
CLARKSON POTTER/PUBLISHERS,
AN IMPRINT OF THE CROWN PUBLISHING GROUP,
A DIVISION OF RANDOM HOUSE, INC., NEW YORK.
WWW.CROWNPUBLISHING.COM
WWW.CLARKSONPOTTER.COM

CLARKSON POTTER IS A TRADEMARK AND POTTER WITH
COLOPHON IS A REGISTERED TRADEMARK OF RANDOM
HOUSE, INC.

GRATEFUL ACKNOWLEDGMENT IS MADE TO GEOFF ARMOUR
FOR PERMISSION TO REPRINT THE POEM "LIBRARY"
FROM *LIGHT ARMOUR* BY RICHARD ARMOUR, COPYRIGHT ©
1954, COPYRIGHT RENEWED 1982 BY RICHARD ARMOUR.
REPRINTED BY PERMISSION OF GEOFF ARMOUR.

LIBRARY OF CONGRESS CATALOGING-IN-PUBLICATION DATA
IS AVAILABLE UPON REQUEST.

ISBN 978-0-307-46132-2

PRINTED IN CHINA

DESIGN BY AMY SLY

PHOTOGRAPHS BY STEVEN RANDAZZO

10 9 8 7 6 5 4 3 2 1

FIRST EDITION

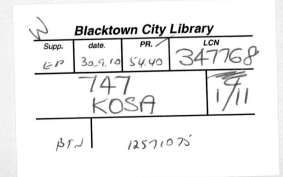

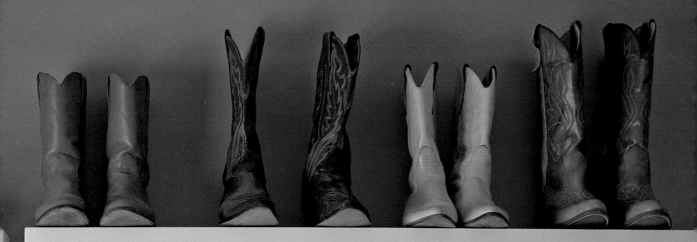

As soon as I enter the house of a new client, I begin noticing the objects that I love to work with as an interior designer—not just beautiful furnishings but also the treasured family possessions that Monica describes throughout this book. It's obvious to me that Monica and I share a very similar philosophy about interior design: a house is not a home unless it displays our most cherished pieces. Full individual expression needs its place in every house, and so does a consciousness of family history, of shared values, of inherited and acquired tastes. These are qualities that cannot be "layered on" like an extra coat of paint. They are integral to the design, for family, friends, and guests to see and experience as they cross your threshold.

I wonder how much of our shared appreciation comes from being raised in families where art, design, and aesthetic tastes were paramount. In my own case, my parents loved to travel. They took scores of photographs, and my late father painted hundreds of watercolors that his friends and family treasure now more than ever. The photographs fill sixty bound volumes that are beautiful objects in and of themselves. They're in my mother's bedroom, along with collections of postcards, each with a short message that fills a line or two, as well as a number of "sayings," each one framed like an epigraph. To stir memories of my own past, and my parents', all I have to do is step into their room and glance around at the intimate interior, or open one of the many albums that speak of those exuberant travels.

Of course, now I have my own collections of images, and though they're fewer in number, I'm definitely continuing the tradition. What else can I do? These are some of the things I value most. Throughout my apartment, photos and watercolor paintings are collected on tabletops, sequestered on walls, and arranged throughout my bedroom, creating landscapes very much like the ones you find pictured in this book. I'm serious about what I love. Like Monica, I believe that these objects, so much a part of our lives, need to be thoroughly integrated into our lives.

Placed on a mirrored coffee table, colorful image cases holding photos remind the family of their travels— red for India and blue for Italy.

As an interior designer, I feel I am most successful working with a family when I am able to help them express their own values, passions, comforts, memories, and lifestyle. That is when the magic happens. Of course I could come into a home, plan each room, and fill it with beautiful objects, but that's not my objective. I want a house that will truly belong to the family, and to achieve that, I need to accommodate those things that are really part of that family's life.

My role is almost that of a curator. The process that we go through, in decorating the room, is very much what you'll be doing when you browse this book and begin thinking up ideas for each area. We let the room speak to us. What's missing? Where is the space just waiting to be occupied by something that will remind us of who we are? Once we see where these things can go, the creative work begins.

I suspect that you'll be going through a similar process as you read this book and begin to jot down ideas and take note of the many solutions that are shown on these pages. Just as I have drawn inspiration from those sixty albums of photographs, you have the opportunity to travel vicariously to the homes shown here. And you can see clearly what they have in common. Though they range from the modest to the spectacular, all bear the unmistakable imprint of their owners' lives and tastes.

In my own house my family enjoys living with some Monica Rich Kosann photographs of my children—the twins, Michalis and Markos (two years old, as I write), and my seven-month-old daughter, Aliki. The children are changing so quickly, I realize I'll see these photographs each day with different eyes. Knowing that I'll want to watch the children grow, as well as remember them at this age, I've even left the frames unsealed, so the photographs can be removed and replaced.

That kind of constant change is inspiring. We get to live with the many images and objects and reminders that fill our present lives and yet, each day, we have new opportunities to reconsider the elements of the family. And eventually, we get to see each home the way it was meant to be—as a place of permanence where experiences are constantly being refreshed and made anew.

Though the ambience is open and bright, the books, photos, important ribbons, and slippers are signs of a personal space where comfort is paramount.

# PREFACE

I caught the photography bug when I was seventeen years old, though, looking back, I can see that the conditions were in place long before then.

Both of my parents are from Europe, but they moved to New York before my sister and I were born. My father was an avid amateur photographer and music buff, and my mother was a dedicated art collector with a wonderful appreciation for artists' new work. Starting out, she used to have "openings" in our home, when she would clear away her personal collection and rehang the public places in the house like the showrooms of a gallery with the work of a single artist. Starting at an early age, my sister and I were often taken to operas and museums. But it was photography that first caught my interest and then became a passion.

For more than twenty years, I have been professionally photographing families, children, and adults. When I take photographs, my objective is to capture a special moment that is not only artistic but also exposes something more telling about the subjects. I had no idea that before long I would find myself dealing with a topic that goes beyond camerawork. But one thing led to another. As I worked with my clients and their children, we would inevitably start to discuss not only the photos themselves but also how they would be framed and where they could be displayed around the home. Many clients asked me to return, especially as their children grew up and their parents aged. The scores of photographs became a visual record of important passages in the family history. Before long, I realized that we were not just discussing photos, frames, and display areas but that, in a larger sense, I was becoming more and more of a family-memory advisor in the art of filling a home with tangible reminders of the family's past and present, assisting with decisions about family albums, keepsakes, and memorabilia as well as frames, photos (old and new), and display areas.

In my own work I became increasingly fascinated with, and influenced by, the turn-of-the-century pictorialist photographers. Their work was the beginning of photography as "art" and not just documentation. I was not only interested in the photographs themselves but also in the beautiful accessories that were used as personal pieces of art during that same period of time. Then I discovered that many of these vintage pieces could still be found in antiques stores and flea markets. My husband and I became frequent visitors to these sites, and before long, I began to search with my clients as well. And then we explored how the things they loved in their own homes—antiques, heirlooms, and collectibles—could be put on display and made part of the family landscape.

Fortunately, I relished this expanded responsibility. We soon moved on to discussions of how they could display things they had inherited from parents or grandparents. They showed me silver pieces engraved with names or initials; craftwork and pieces of art passed along from one generation to the next; travel souvenirs; heirlooms; as well as their collections. Sometimes, a single inherited object would become the inspiration for a new collection—creating the new from the old.

I'm always happy when I return to a family that I've photographed over the years, see how the kids have grown, catch up on the latest family news, and also—quite often—discover how the family has added elements to their home that are uniquely reflective of their lives. In my own home, living with "things" from my life continually inspires me.

Though the scope of my work has broadened, the themes have remained constant. What I call "the fine art of family" is far more than taking photographs and hanging them on the wall, or finding the right place for an old heirloom. Each of us has the power to transform our personal living space into an area where family memories are kept alive, where we pay respect to our values and accomplishments, express our tastes, communicate our enthusiasms, and create the memories and experiences that friends, relatives, and children will forever associate with the place we call home. There is, indeed, an art to it. And that art is what this book is all about.

As I remind my clients, cherished objects are not just a thing of the past. Whenever we take a photograph, add a personal touch to something that belongs to us, or select a new piece for a collection, we are in the process of *creating* heirlooms for others. Of course, we can't say what will become of these or which of them will be most valued by future generations, but that's all the more reason to take personal pleasure in the family landscape. Bring them into the light, and always be ready to express your memories and add your personal touch.

—MONICA RICH KOSANN

# INTRODUCTION
## PLEASE REMEMBER THIS

Footfalls echo in the memory
Down the passage which we did not take
Towards the door we never opened
Into the rose-garden.
—T. S. ELIOT, "BURNT NORTON," *FOUR QUARTETS*

No MATTER WHERE YOU LIVE OR HOW big your home is, your photographs, heirlooms, and collectibles are part of your life. They help to convey your heritage, your family history, and at the same time, they are very much part of your present and future life. Today, in your own home, you are engaged in the act and the art of creating memories for yourself, your family, your relatives, and everyone who visits your home. How can you do that most effectively and creatively?

There are, indeed, some strategies. You're making an artistic statement when you bring these objects out into the open and show them off. They may be beautiful on their own, but they are also evocative. They suggest memories and generate emotions. Of course, you can always bring out an heirloom, dust it off, and find some place for it. But in this book, I'd like to give you some tips on doing more than that. What will make that object look good in your environment? How can you give these possessions a meaningful place, or create a collection that has a whole new meaning?

Some people seem to avoid bringing out heirlooms for fear that they turn a home into an historical museum or a gallery. It doesn't have to be that way. Create a space that you want to live in. You can bring memories alive, and create a sense of family history, in ways that express your passions and reflect your tastes. No need for mustiness and cobwebs. Family heirlooms deserve respect, of course, but the key is to integrate them into your everyday life. And, as I've pointed out, any object that has been imprinted in some way with the touch of your personality or the mark of your ownership becomes, in itself, an heirloom for future generations.

In the pages ahead, while I'm showing how family photos can be framed and hung, I'll also provide many other ideas about the ways you can use family furniture, memorabilia, souvenirs from trips and vacations, and the other tangible reminders of who you are, where you came from, and what your experiences have been. I'll invite you

to peer into kitchens, bedrooms, studies, and libraries where many families have surrounded themselves and their household members with evocative antiques, flea-market finds, art, and memorabilia. You'll see how some people have started collections that grew and grew, while others have been inspired to launch careers, take up new pursuits, and seek out fresh contacts in pursuit of their enthusiasms. I hope this will prove to be for you—as it has been for me—a journey of discovery.

But for all the inspiring examples in this book, I urge you to follow your own instincts and do it your way. Just as no family is quite like mine or yours, there's really no such thing as a recipe for the way you express yourself in the domain of your own home. The space you occupy deserves to be filled with its own images, echoes, and signings. Your home is like no other. Why not fill it with reminders, at every turn, that this is so?

PREVIOUS PAGES A threesome of French ceramic developing trays—a thoughtful gift from a client—holds artifacts of my life as a photographer, mom, and flea-market aficionado.
ABOVE In a beachside cottage, a worn table is appropriate for holding a collection of handmade and store-bought boxes.
OPPOSITE A miniature "history-to-go" occupies a single tray with a collection of family images in sterling-silver frames, vintage and new, in all shapes and sizes.

# MIXING THE OLD
# AND THE NEW

Throughout our house, my husband and I have photographs of our parents, grandparents, children, and more distant relatives that are completely mixed in with photos that are much more recent. The point is to remind all of us that family is family, no matter which generation. When photos are intermingled this way, it helps bring up conversations about cultural history, reminding kids (especially) that they share a family life with parents, great-grandparents, and great-great-grandparents. To further the sense of timelessness and continuity, I often put recent photographs in antique frames or, conversely, get brand-new frames for photos that are yellowed with age.

As I look around, I see that our home does indeed have a personal stamp on it. The whole range of objects—from my children's art projects to porcelain pieces, old cameras, vintage boxes and cases, photographs, and numerous other items—have their own places in my studio, where I spend so much of my time. These are the personal touches and statements that remind me of one home that is not like any other. In fact, some of my ancestors I know best only through their images. With some of these ancestors I find myself looking for clues to who they were, with little to go on except their garb, their posture, and their surroundings. For example, I have a picture of my mother's father, Josef, who died when my mother was three or four years old. In the age-tinged photograph, I see a young Austrian gentleman in old Vienna standing alongside his classic Badge motorcycle. He wears a rakish cap with a narrow, black brim, his goggles perched on top like the eyes of a frog. What a sight! Vest, tie, jodhpurs, the whole bit—he's obviously posed, a cigarette in hand, looking prepared to break some land-speed record and, after that, take on the world. And instead? Instead, he is the father my mother lost, the grandfather I would never know, the hint of the shadow of a clue to my own beginnings. And this portrait is all I have!

In every home, I think, there need to be places where family photographs, heirlooms, and collectibles can be displayed. The first step is to find some of these items where they're stored or hidden away in different areas around your home. The next step is to bring them out of hiding and to begin to consider the spaces where they can go in your home. Let's begin with the photographs.

OPPOSITE In my studio, a vintage dental chest was drafted into service for holding clients' work, favorite portraits, and memorabilia.

# WHERE ARE YOU HIDING YOUR KODAK MOMENTS?

When Kodak introduced the first easy-to-use, handheld box camera in 1888, the advertising slogan was "You Press the Button, We Do the Rest." Like most advertising taglines, this was a gross exaggeration. Yes, the box camera was easy to use, and it caught on. Families at home or on vacation started to carry it everywhere, snapping photographs of Aunt Sally and Uncle Jim in front of their first Model-T, or Sister Susie and Cousin Jane in the garden. For family occasions there were the obligatory posed photographs, with everyone dressed to the nines and smiling for the camera, standing stiffly until the family's designated photographer finally pushed the button and said, "Okay, we're done."

Part of the Kodak slogan was, in fact, quite true. If the intrepid family photographer unloaded the film and delivered it to the drugstore or post office, Kodak did its part and returned the prints. In many families the delivery was eagerly anticipated. When the photographs arrived, they were passed around and pored over. The box camera was, indeed, an innovative family-memory device. It captured moments that would never be lost. Kodak had performed a great service.

But in creating this most convenient of family-memory accessories, Kodak—soon followed by other companies—also gave birth to a monster. At first the monster was just a stack of photographs in a binder or two. Before long, the stack grew to occupy boxes. Then drawers. Then whole shelves. All across America, and then the world, family photographs were stacked, stored, boxed, moved, and, as time went on, passed down from genera-

tion to generation. And as technology advanced, so did the vast oversupply of family photos until, today, they occupy nooks, crannies, and closet spaces. And with the advent of digital photography, millions of images got stored away in cyberspace. So, now, in addition to foraging through the house for photos we'd like to display, there's the further challenge of scouring digital archives.

Kodak did indeed fulfill its advertised promise to build the camera, create the film, and handle the processing. But as for "the rest"? Well—that's all up to us.

In my own photography work I like the shots that "capture the moment." The best, to me, is the photo that finds people when their guard is down, when they are expressing themselves or relating to each other or to their environment rather than posing for the camera. But I also want to emphasize, right here, that this is an artistic and personal preference. True, any selection of family photos requires you to make certain choices. But throughout this book, I want to make my message clear: It is more important to choose what you love, whether it's a photograph that was professionally commissioned or one that you took on a special day.

The same can be said of the heirlooms and collectibles that you bring out of storage and into the light. Some will evoke an instant response, perhaps because they're associated with a particular person who was important to you, or perhaps because it brings back good memories. Go by your instincts. Even if something looks like it could be, or should be, a "valuable piece," that's not the best reason to make it part of your family landscape. To earn that right, it needs to mean something more.

OPPOSITE I have drawers filled with Victorian-era studio cards, portraits glued onto cardboard backings. While my own photos emphasize intimacy and spontaneity, these old studio cards are literally "still-life" photographs, because the subjects had to sit immobile while the pictures were being taken.

# ALL ON THE
# FAMILY WALL

In Socrates' renowned allegory, the Greek philosopher describes a cave where captive viewers can see only shadows on a wall. Behind where the viewers are sitting, all sorts of real-life figures are passing back and forth, chatting, moving around, having celebrations and funerals, doing whatever people do in real life. But all the viewers can see are the shadows of the real figures projected on the far wall of the cave.

When I walk into a hallway filled with family photos, I sometimes feel like one of the viewers whom Socrates described, viewing shadows on a wall. I stop to look closely at the photo of a young boy or girl; or the portrait of a grandmother; kids at a birthday party; dogs romping in a yard—and the images transport me into another world. It's a world in which I have never actually been. I may not even know who these people are, when they lived, or what they were up to. But I see the moments of their lives, caught forever in two dimensions.

Alas, in many homes, walls are empty. Wasted space! This is one of those areas in the home that begs to be used—and not just for wallpaper, framed prints, mirrors, or painted landscapes. Walls are prime territory for all the flickering shadows of family memories. Here, you can remind your own children what they looked like when they were little. They can see for themselves how they've changed and how they've remained the same. Walls can remind them of new friends who have come into their lives and of family they'll remember forever.

Children can view their complete family history on your walls. If you had ancestors who came by boat from the Old World, crossed the plains by prairie schooner, went off to war, wore bowlers and straw hats, held picnics on sunny lawns, traveled to amusement parks on weekends or to beaches and forest on vacations, this is where you can admire their ways and recall their habits. All the differences between *right now* and *back then* can be displayed (in any order you wish) along the walls of a hallway. And these are sights for anyone to see. Whether you're a guest in someone else's house, a family member, a connoisseur of history, or a lover of nostalgia, family walls create a wonderful place to pause, browse, wonder, laugh, and remember.

A wall display doesn't need to be dedicated to nostalgic memories, though. Any wall can also display a quirky or fun collection.

**PREVIOUS PAGES** On the wall of his stairway, Eric Cohler—a collector of fine-art photography—has used his archival prints to create a "family wall" landscape. His collection includes some of the great portrait photographers ranging from Cartier-Bresson to Bert Stern.

ABOVE The space above a couch is usually reserved for artwork, but in this front foyer, a passionate collector of antique weathervanes displays, instead, a varied sampling of animal-shaped vanes rescued from the tops of old barns and houses.

# WHERE TO BEGIN

In many homes families use their walls and hall-ways with great ingenuity and creativity. Results are highly individualistic. I'll show some of those displays to help you get started, but please don't get hung up on the idea that you need an overall plan before you begin. Many of these collections just evolved, and if they now look thought out and orga-nized, that's because the owners have been willing to move pieces around, replace them, rehang them, put old ones away, and add some new.

That said, it *can* be tough to get started. Whether you're hanging the first family picture in a long, dim hallway or just beginning to fill a vast space in a brightly lit living room, the first frame is going to look very lonely and out of place. Even a grouping of photos may look, at first, like a lonely atoll in a vast ocean. If you have the instincts of an orga-nizer, you might have to fight your own impulse to impose order before you've even begun.

My initial advice, then, is to give it time. Once the process starts, you'll find a natural growth. The collections I love best are often very disorderly and nonchronological. But that's part of the plea-sure. Images on a wall are almost a Rorschach test of a family's relationships, values, and heritage. The growth of such a collection should be evolu-tionary. And if you hesitate for even a moment when you're starting the memory wall, just remind yourself of this: What if *no one* ever saw these pic-tures? How much would be lost?

OPPOSITE A home office has been turned into a room that is welcoming and comfortable, celebrating the owner's passion for golf and his affection for his family.

LEFT From newborn to young child, one girl has been portrayed by many artists—in watercolor, oil, charcoal, and photographs—each expressing a unique imaginative approach.

## MIX YOUR MEDIA

In truth, nothing captures our attention like images of ourselves. But images are ever changing. At some point I think we all realize that each of us is seen in different ways by different people.

Recently I took photographs of a young girl. When the family showed me where they planned to hang them, I was intrigued by what they had created over the years on their walls. There were a number of other photos, including a black-and-white taken when she was probably eleven months old and a very stylized Andy Warhol–style color photo that must have been done when

she was five or six. But what really struck me was the adventurous way this family used a variety of media to portray their child. There were pen-and-ink drawings, oil paintings, and charcoal sketches along with many other black-and-white and color photographs in a range of styles. This was a family to whom art was important. Just looking at the wonderful array of representations, I realized how much they were teaching their children, not just about seeing themselves, but about the many ways they could be seen by others. It was such a perfect way for the parents to convey their love of art as well as their love for their children.

# LET A
# HALLWAY SPEAK
# TO YOUR KIDS

If your family life is anything like mine, there are precious few times when you talk to your kids about the importance of family life, family history, or your heritage. Yet these are things that we, as adults, do value enormously. So how do we communicate that?

Does your home have a hallway connecting bedrooms? Think of the number of times your family members travel that corridor, oblivious to their environment.

Create what I call the Happy Hallway. Its message may be subliminal, but eventually kids do get it. In the middle of an argument, maybe they'll look up and see some picture of themselves a few years ago, laughing and holding hands and playing ring-around-the-rosy. Racing to catch the bus, they just might notice that family photograph of some special moment when one of them was hugging Mom or being lifted in the air by Dad.

Who knows what sticks? What we do know is that images have impact. From their earliest days, kids are bombarded with images created by advertising, by the media, by the Internet, by product creators and marketers. In your own home there are limited marketing opportunities, but the Happy Hallway is one of them. This is the place to make your pitch for all the good feelings associated with family. Whether they "get it" or not, at least your kids will *see* it daily. The evidence of family happiness is right there.

"Our children grow up in worlds that are different from ours," observes family psychologist Daniel Gottlieb in his book *Voices in the Family*. "They see the world initially through our eyes, our spouse's eyes, and their older siblings' eyes. And then they develop eyes of their own."

The Happy Hallway is designed for that moment when they develop eyes of their own.

LEFT When photographs are framed like this—with identical dark frames and white matting—the image becomes the focal point.

# TIPS ON CHOOSING NEW FRAMES

If you are framing an heirloom piece of art or a photograph you want to preserve and hang on the wall, one option is to work with a professional framer. You know you have found the right place if they offer conservation or museum-quality framing. For the photos on display in my own home, I select frames as carefully as I would for my gallery shows.

All the materials used in framing should be acid-free. That means, literally, there are no acidic materials touching the photograph or piece of art that cause discoloration or deterioration over the years.

I always advise clients to find a framer they like to work with and return to that person (if you can) every time you have a framing job. It helps to have someone who already has an idea of your tastes and preferences when you come in the door. Helpful suggestions from an expert framer can make the whole process of selection much easier.

Here are some of the basics you'll need to know when you're working with a framer.

» The artwork will be supported by an acid-free board, which is the very light but stiff backing on which it's mounted.

» The *mat board* (or simply *mat*) is also acid-free and it comes in various thickness. My framer likes to use an eight-ply cotton rag mat, which is expensive, but four-ply is fine as well. The mat goes on top of the art, with a *window* cut in the center to reveal the photograph. The inside of the window usually has a *beveled edge*; it's cut at a 45-degree angle to help draw the viewer's eye to the image in the center.

» Frames, of course, come in a multitude of shapes and sizes, and a frame shop will be able to show you hundreds of alternatives. Don't be afraid to be creative. If you trust your framer, ask for recommendations, at least to get you started. Wood, metal, and plastic frames are available. For my own photographs I most often choose a very simple white, silver, or black wood frame.

» A prominent element of the frame is the *molding*, the shaped or decorated outer edge of the frame. Here's where my framer and I spend a lot of time going through choices. The goal? To find a molding that can work hand in hand with the soul of the image.

» Other features of the frame are the *rabbet* (the inner lip of the frame that holds all the framing materials) and the *dust cover* (the sealed paper on the back that keeps out dust, dirt, and insects).

» You'll have a choice of which glass or *glazing* to select. The most expensive and best glass—both for viewing and for protecting the art—is museum quality. It completely blocks out ultraviolet (UV) rays to preserve the artwork, and it also has anti-reflective qualities so the viewer won't be distracted by glare. While you may not select this top-of-the-line glass for every piece, it's advisable to always get UV-blocking glass for any work that you want to preserve. All quality framers will carry it.

» An alternative way to frame a picture is to "float" the image in a box frame. (The mounted photographs in the living areas shown on page 36 were done this way.) The image doesn't need to be matted. The framer will use archival tape to mount the photo so it looks like it's floating in a shadow box.

# A FAMILY TREE IN
# PHOTOGRAPHS

What happens when a child born at the turn of the twenty-first century holds the gaze of a great-great-great-grandparent who lived 120 years previously? Such things, unfortunately, don't happen in real life. But they can happen in any room of the house. I've seen family photographs in dressing rooms and closets, foyers, sitting rooms, and on bathroom walls. Every part of the house is an eligible display area.

ABOVE Here's an alternative way to make a wall display with family photos, using a mélange of frames from different eras to match the subjects.

ABOVE Greeted by muted overhead lighting and mellow walls, visitors feel welcomed to this private family gallery at the end of a hallway.

For each of us, the story of how we came into being is the unending story. Fortunately, we are free to create endless versions of that complex and confusing tale. Chronology doesn't matter. I love to see a wall that looks like a family tree where the branches have been trimmed off and scattered around. You can pause in front of a smiling, full-busted woman in a hairnet who's standing in a kitchen in front of her stove, and almost smell the tomato sauce cooking. Right next to her is a young girl in a dancing outfit, learning her first steps. These two photographs are separated by many years. What is the connection? Who are these people and how are they linked?

Anyone with a storehouse of family photographs has the resources to create what I call the Fine Art of Family Wall. Images from the distant past are mixed with those from the present day. Formal portraits take their place next to candid snapshots, as if the differences in generations could be made to vanish. But somewhere in the family there are always people who know some of the events, connections, and characters, and can tell stories about what is shown in the photographs. This wall is a living testimonial to the family's past, present, and future. And a great place for the storytelling to begin.

ABOVE Flat-screen TV monitors set into the wall display an endless combination of images. This same effect can be achieved on a smaller scale with smaller digital frames now widely available.

## GO HIGH TECH

With the many possibilities of digital display, it's possible to choose from a nearly infinite variety of screens—self-standing or wall mounted—of every conceivable size. And the images on those screens can reach as far back in time as your own technological know-how will permit. Even old prints or paintings can be digitally reproduced with a high degree of accuracy. You can upload a series of digital photographs that can be changed or replaced as often as you wish—or create an ever-changing display that can be sequenced in any order.

While I prefer the resolution and quality of print photography in my own home, I have seen digital display used beautifully to create a memory wall where several large display monitors along one wall show large-scale photos of family. The patiently timed fade-ins and fade-outs place images on each screen just long enough to appreciate before one is replaced by the next. Walking the well-lit hallway is like discovering, greeting, and passing an array of family memories, all in transition. It's an entrancing use of this technology.

## GO SMALL

Some children take great delight in anything that's miniature—a doll-house; toy trucks, cars, and trains; or tiny replicas of towns and land-scapes. There's some of that magic in looking at miniature portraits. You have to come up very close, focus on the image, and when you do, it's almost like looking through a keyhole and seeing someone staring directly back into your eyes.

An expanse of very small photographs can make a stunning display, as shown here. Designer Rita Konig's collection of Polaroid snapshots forms

**LEFT** Looking casually taped-on, with edges curled, a symmetrical array of well-aligned Polaroids is the visual centerpiece of a small apartment.
**ABOVE** Including an "imperfection" in an otherwise symmetrical display is the art of wabi-sabi.

a large expanse of mixed images above the fireplace. To register what's going on, you have to step very close. Each of those Polaroids is an instant of personal history—and there are hundreds to look at. Together, they create a colorful landscape comprised of miniatures, but it's really a single narrative about one woman's life and interests.

Working with miniatures like this is a great way to give visitors a glimpse into moments of a family's story. If you have limited space, you can arrange these small photographs to create a narrative or just add more snapshots when you get them, expanding outward from the center. So the display not only conveys history, but also everything that's fresh and new in your life and your travels.

If you put miniatures in frames, you create a different kind of effect. The collection of small images in a master bedroom shown at right occupies a narrow wall area near the corner of the room next to sliding glass doors. When my friend BJ and her family moved from her previous home to this one, she took the entire collection and rehung it in her bedroom. She said that she needed to do that before she really felt as if she had moved in to her new home.

Unlike Rita's vast collection of unframed Polaroids, every photo in this collection is carefully framed, and each frame complements the portrait that it contains. The vintage frames are flea-market finds while the others were made by her children. Each photograph has a well-considered place on the narrow wall, and each frame is special because of the way she found the frame or who gave it to her.

RIGHT Each mini-photo is adhered to the mat with acid-free tape and appears to float in a 1½-inch-thick box frame.

LEFT Like beads on strings, the images of family from the recent and distant past stretch from ceiling to floor on a narrow wall.
ABOVE Handmade frames from faraway places can dress up vacation snapshots, as well as formal studio photographs.

This approach creates a random, personal feeling that invites conversation. But there are other approaches if you want to create a more simple, orderly display of photographs to suit your design sensibilities. For instance, a simple gridlike arrangement—with all photographs in identical frames—works very well on a large wall, especially if you have a contemporary décor with clean-lined furnishing and unpatterned wall treatments. The grid arrangement could be square—for instance, three rows of three—or rectangular, with a vertical or horizontal orientation. When all the pictures are framed identically, your eye is drawn to the images themselves. The result is more for-

mal, like a gallery or museum display, but it invites the viewer to give unbiased attention to every image in the "grid."

Another structured approach that works particularly well on a long wall is "railroading" the images. You literally create two tracks of identically framed photos, one above and one below, that invite the viewer to move along, image by image, absorbing them in sequence. As with the grid approach, identical frames give equal weight to every picture in the lineup, but the two-track arrangement suggests a rationale behind the sequence—either a chronological development or the exploration of a theme.

# GO LARGE

You can achieve a bold, dramatic effect with just one photograph that dominates a room. Less is more. If you decide to scale up, though, you need to carefully choose the image. The attention-grabbing photograph will have a distinct impact on your environment. A recent snapshot of your kids or a studio-quality photograph of your anniversary may be a wonderful addition to a wall that's crowded with a scattershot array of photographs, but if you're going to enlarge one photo to fit into a larger frame, be selective.

Of all the wall treatments, a single, very large photograph makes a provocative statement. It demands attention. If you have a family photograph that's also a terrific piece of art, frame it like a gallery piece and hang it where it will get maximum attention. You need an image that the family loves and that guests can enjoy as well as admire. Consider a number of criteria:

» WHAT'S THE MOOD OF THE PHOTO?

There's nothing more touching than someone caught in a thoughtful or reflective pose. But a look conveys a mood. Before placing that kind of portrait prominently in a living room, recreation room, or dining room, think about the impact it will have. Since this will be a photo that you're living with every day, consider the artistic appeal. You want an image that has good aesthetic qualities as well as personal significance.

» IS THERE ACTION IN THE PICTURE?

A high-quality black-and-white portrait photo can be both impressive and arresting to the viewer. Think of the subject of that portrait—regardless of his or her relationship to you—as a presence in the room. If you display a photograph where there's motion, interaction, and energy, that will be transmitted into the atmosphere of the room.

» IS IT EXPRESSIVE?

Often, the best photograph for a dominant position is one that is dynamic. The image needs to sustain your interest daily, which means you might be more comfortable with a somewhat mysterious shot than with a simple "action shot." One of the joys of art is being able to find something new in a piece every time you return to it, and the same holds true of any large-scale photograph. You want a work that captures not only a particular moment or conjures up a memory in the life of your family or loved one but also expresses an emotion that you want to share with anyone who enters the room. (A good example is the huge portrait of three boys shown here. It's seven feet high and leaning, unframed, against a wall. But it demands attention, and the energy of that portrait fills the room.)

» DOES IT INVITE ATTENTION?

You know you've selected the right picture if your guests immediately ask, "Who *is* that?" And when you reply, "That's my daughter," or "That's my son," their reaction is, "When was that taken? I've never seen that before!" A large image should, by its very nature, be a conversation piece. If it draws attention and generates discussion, then it's definitely working in that space.

OPPOSITE This life-size blowup of a digital photograph is a C-print mounted on aluminum and coated with UV protection.

# A HOME WHERE THE WALLS TELL A STORY

**Some time ago, I got my first call from Fanny, a young woman who has three daughters. Fanny and her husband wanted some photographs to hang in their home and to send as Christmas cards. The girls were several years apart in age, and the youngest, at that point, was just under two years old. Fanny asked whether I could come to her house to try to get the three girls together. What I didn't anticipate was the beginning of a wonderful relationship with this warm, ebullient woman and her delightful daughters that—as I write—is now in its twelfth year.**

When I first came to their house, I wondered how the family photographs I was taking would be displayed in their home. In a traditional home, there are an infinite number of places where family photographs, heirlooms, and memorabilia can be displayed. While their home felt open, warm, and welcoming, I noted that the spacious wall areas had no paintings, prints, or photographs. The elegant, comfortable furniture had clean, simple lines, but I saw no signs of family antiques or heirlooms. In that vast, beautiful modern house with its careful layout and wide-open spaces, where would these photos go? Would they, after all, be put away in photo albums or efficiently filed and stored for later viewing?

Characteristically, Fanny had a vision of what she wanted. When I brought over the proofs, we eagerly began the selection process. We both instinctively gravitated toward the images that, to me, held aesthetic appeal and were fully expressive of her daughters' emotional lives.

OPPOSITE In an Aspen home with cathedral ceilings, spot lighting and symmetrical placement heighten the dramatic effect of family photographs.

After the initial selection had been made, Fanny and her interior designer, Lisa Monteleone, paid a visit to my studio, where the three of us worked together, discussing subject, size, placement, and the arrangement of horizontals and verticals. We talked through each detail: Can this image be bigger? What do you think of this print? If we put these two photos of the girls side by side, what are the other images going to be and where do we place them? It was a collaboration of the best kind.

Once I'd made the prints to the specified sizes, Lisa arranged for the prints to be mounted between two layers of glass. The way the photographs are mounted in the specially designed frames makes them appear suspended in midair, with the wall visible behind. Each photograph appears to be floating within its frame.

The result is a bold and unconventional way to display family photographs. In the living room, a number of framed prints dominates the wall space above the couch. Any first-time visitor to that room seeing photographs of the daughters would immediately wonder, "Who are those happy girls? What's the story here?" And would be told, "These

RIGHT As the children grow, their parents change the photographs that are mounted between glass. OPPOSITE A love of family and a love of the outdoors—both are blended in this dining room where there are photographs of the family.

are our daughters!" What a tribute to them all.

As time goes by and Fanny replaces the older prints with new photographs of her daughters, visitors are greeted with an ever-changing kaleidoscope of their growing up. Prints are displayed with just as much prominence in the dining room, in the kitchen, in the hallways, in the family room, in the bathroom—virtually everywhere in the house.

Clearly, this family's home is as unique as their lifestyle, but what they have done with their family pictures is something that anyone can do in his or her own home. By choice, they portray their daughters with images that convey the warmth and spontaneity that they all share. And the way they display these photos on the walls of every living area is not only a sign of their personal taste and energetic approach to life. Those photos are also a testament to their very concept of happiness.

# VOLUMES OF
# MEMORIES

Here is where people,
One frequently finds,
Lower their voices
And raise their minds.
—RICHARD ARMOUR, "LIBRARY"

Aside from being a place to house books, libraries can be sanctuaries from a busy world. You can let yourself be transported to a faraway place in a story, or you can sit meditatively reflecting on your life. Any room in the house—or, for that matter, any *corner* of a room— can be turned into a personal library. Of course books themselves are a rich font of memories, especially if their pages have been turned time and again through the years.

How can you transform your own library— whatever its dimensions—into a special place that's alive with memories? I've seen it done many ways.

## SHELVES ARE FOR
## MORE THAN BOOKS

In a public or academic library, most shelves are filled to capacity with . . . just books. There's no reason why your home library needs to look that way. The shelves are made-to-order display areas for personal photographs that can remind you of places you've been, times that you've enjoyed, or of past family get-togethers. While these photos may have a very private meaning to you—evoking a unique time or place or celebration—I think you'll find that other family members (especially children) become curious about the scenes that are represented, and they'll ask you to share your memories.

PREVIOUS PAGES In a newly renovated shorefront stone house, the grand entrance to the library is flanked by hand-painted screens that express the owners' love of Chinese art.
ABOVE A deep green art nouveau bookend offers a colorful contrast to the dark wood shelf of the library.

**ABOVE** Candid photographs of spirited moments hold places of honor in the family library when professionally framed.

Shelves are such a flexible display area. Just pull out a few books to make a space, and you have room for a family portrait, a landscape, or an heirloom photograph. If a picture frame is freestanding, it can be placed near the front of the shelf. Others can be propped against bookends or the back wall. You may want to form a pairing or small grouping on a single shelf. Or tap a picture hook into the outside edge of a shelf and hang the photo there. When you want to move photos to a different part of the library, it's easy. No measuring or centering needed. Just choose a different shelf, move aside some books, and presto, you have a new display area.

## PLACE PICTURES AT EVERY HEIGHT

When family members or visitors come to your library, what's the first thing they see? What are the memories you would like them to know about, ask about, or share?

Given floor-to-ceiling shelves, you have hundreds of square feet to work with. Some photos can be placed at eye level to catch the attention of someone just passing through. For young children, you'll want some of your family photos on the lower shelves, by which the kids may sit reading or playing games. (I find that it doesn't take long before children get curious about old photographs—particularly if they're of someone they know—and begin asking who took the photo, and when, and where.)

RIGHT Picture hooks at the edges of the shelves hold the framed photos, which can be easily moved anywhere in the home library.

# SEARCHING FOR VINTAGE FRAMES

To find the right frames for your photographs—especially old family photos—it can be fun to scour flea markets and antiques stores or go online. Look for a variety of shapes and sizes in stained or natural wood, gilded, silver, or black, with interesting moldings, engravings, and ornamentation.

When I'm matching a frame to a photograph, I'm likely to linger quite a while, trying various photos in different frames until I find the match that pleases me. (See the resources section, pages 181–184, for antiques and flea-market locations.) You may not have a particular photograph in mind when you spot a vintage frame that appeals to you, but even so, if you like it and the price is right, bring it home. Eventually, you'll find a photo that fits.

Here are some guidelines to keep in mind when you're browsing:

» Be on the lookout for round frames, especially for baby photographs. There's nothing cuter than a cherubic baby face in a little round frame. A round frame also works well if you intend to crop a photograph, selecting one face or figure from a larger photo. The round frame creates a spy-hole effect that really focuses attention on the portrait.

» Squares and rectangles are more classic, and if you get a large enough frame, the photograph may fit without any cropping. If you get a frame that's much larger than the photo, you can always add a mat to fill out the area between the image and the frame. (Matting a photo gives it more importance.)

» Don't reject a frame because the glass is broken, the back is damaged, or the stand is missing. All these things can be repaired. A glass cutter or framer can replace the glass; an unsightly or stained backing can be replaced; and if the frame doesn't have a stand, it can be set on a small easel. As long as you like the molding and it's in good shape, everything else can be fixed.

» If you come across an oval frame, I recommend that you buy it. Ovals are more rare, and they look beautiful standing among other shapes on an antique table or sideboard.

» The most important element is the molding. Does it appeal to you? Do you like its shape? Will it work with your décor? If you have a modern, clean design

OPPOSITE With richly toned wood and distinctively shaped contours, these vintage Scandanavian fruitwood frames seem to speak to one another.

ABOVE The family photographs and memorabilia on the desk are in perfect harmony with the framed original photographic prints on the far wall. Though the family pictures and the artwork occupy different dimensions in this room, all the frames have been given equal attention to make sure they work with the photos.

in your home, look for simple frames, perhaps with silver, black, wood, or glass moldings. For a home with ornate furniture or antiques, you'll want more romantic-looking frames in warmer tones—for example, a richly toned wood, gold, or brass.

» Leather frames look good in many environments, from a dark-toned library to a contemporary living room.

» Occasionally, you'll find frames made of "exotic" materials such as alligator, python, or stingray skin. These can work in any room.

» When you're looking at antique cigarette cases and powder compacts, ask yourself whether they could be used as frames for small photographs. Many can be. Just remember you will have to spend some time cleaning them up before they'll be usable.

» If you see a mirror frame that you like and it's the right size, don't hesitate. The frame will be

perfectly usable once you remove the mirror and replace it with glass.

» Before mounting a picture in a vintage frame, consider having it done by a professional framer, especially if parts need to be repaired or the frame was expensive.

» If you decide to do it yourself, you can visit a do-it-yourself framing shop or go online for framing materials. (See the resources section, pages 181–184 for website addresses.) Carefully pull out the nails that hold the backing, remove the old print or photograph, and lift out the glass. (Be patient, especially if the frame is brittle and the nails are rusty!) If the glass is intact, use it as a template. Trim the photo to fit, make a photocopy, or have it sized at a photo store. If you have a digital print, you can just measure the frame and then scale down the photo to fit.

# CHOOSE PHOTOS THAT
# HELP YOU DAYDREAM

The library that my husband, the kids, and I all share is a sanctuary that holds numerous fond memories of friends and family. My husband is an avid reader, and we have an extensive collection of books on art, design, and photography. When I am working on a new design, or looking for inspiration before visiting a client's home, sometimes I'll just settle into the library and scan the shelves for inspiration. And when I look up from my comfy armchair, there are photos of my family. I see the portrait of my father as a six-year-old and, just a glance away, a picture of my mother when she was eighteen or nineteen. She looks like a movie star. And there are my daughters! And here's where the daydreaming begins. . . .

I remember exactly how and when I took the library photos of my daughters shown on page 47. We were on a trip through Europe. One was taken alongside a river on a dismal day. She appears in a kind of ethereal haze, the river behind her, as if she were floating in another world. That was magical in itself. Better yet was the way we got there, in one of those trains that winds its way through the Alps, giving us breathtaking views of snowcapped mountains and rushing mountain streams. As the train clickety-clacked around cliffs and through passes, I took a second photo. My other daughter was blowing a huge bubble. I remember she was so annoying—sitting there in the compartment, chewing like crazy until finally I said, "Can you *not* chew gum like that?" Her response? She blew an enormous bubble that popped right in my face. But just before she did . . . I lifted the camera, shot the picture. Frozen in time—the teenage daughter; the big, fat, in-your-face bubble; and outside the window, the blurred glory of the countryside rushing past.

Sometimes at night, when the house is completely still, I get into the armchair and pull out some of my favorite photography books to browse under the lamplight. But when I look up, there are my daughters on that miracle of a trip. All time stops, and I'm back there, again, with memories of standing alongside the misty river or traveling on the speeding train that barrels down the mountainside.

Some libraries are designed to keep you away from distractions. But as you can tell, I advocate the opposite. Put the distractions right there, within eyesight, where a glance away from the book you are reading will provide the best fodder for daydreams and memories.

OPPOSITE Clustered around the hearth, dark-hued objects like carved eagles and rustic walking sticks add elegance and warmth to the setting.

## BRING IN THE ARTIFACTS

Displaying family photographs is one way to keep the things we cherish at the forefront of our minds, but there are many other mementoes and memorabilia that people have brought into their reading rooms to keep cherished memories alive. In the spirit of "think outside the box," I would urge you,

in this case, to "think outside the library." Beyond books, art, pens, paper, and the usual library stuff, there are scores of family artifacts that really do belong in a place where, at first blush, they have no business being.

On the mantel shelf in the library of a family friend (see above and on page 54) stands a row of alert and expectant cast-iron animals—among them two bears, a bison, and a turtle—each with a little slot to accept a coin from a child's hand. This

is a piggy bank collection that started with one of the cast-iron pieces that was given to my friend by his father. From that came the collection that he displays in his home office and library. A glance at this collection is an instant reminder of his father. The pocket change that he carefully dropped in those cast-iron animals grew and grew, as did his respect for his father's steady counsel.

Today, this is the library of a very successful businessman, but also someone who has never for a moment forgotten where he came from and what it took to achieve the luxuries he now enjoys. On the desk in that same library is the miniature replica of a town hall, which seems out of place . . . until you learn that this is the town hall that stood next to the grocery store where my friend, as a teenager, spent innumerable hours packing groceries. And nearby, on his desk, looking equally out of place, is an empty shaving mug. Of course there's a story behind this, too. It belonged to his father, the shaving mug he used to lather up every morning. Shaving soap and boar-bristle brush are gone now, but the spirit of the father who inspired his son is very much present in this room.

TOP No ordinary piggy banks, the cast-iron animals on this mantel held the first earnings of a young boy. ABOVE Though cracked and chipped, this shaving mug is an integral part of the room—all the more precious in its owner's eyes because of its flaws.

LEFT A mixture of styles works beautifully to give this library a unique personality, expressed by mixing period pieces with painted bookcases and geometrically patterned carpeting. Though it has the feel of the French art-deco period, the room is anchored by a mantel that comes from a Louis XVI château.

ABOVE For a family whose home interior is as ambitious as their worldwide destinations, bright red bookcases are appropriate for holding their travel books.

# KEEP YOUR TRAVEL MEMORIES ALIVE

If you love to travel, you don't need any lessons in home furnishing or interior design to help create an ideal reading room. This is the place for maps, charts, postcards, stubs of travel tickets, a well-worn suitcase filled with photographs, or a treasured souvenir haggled over with some street vendor. This is also a perfect place to keep the tools that help you prepare for future adventures, a gateway to future voyages.

How you personalize such a library, and what you want to show, is entirely your choice. Perhaps well-thumbed guidebooks from journeys past. Or albums holding the snapshots you took on the sunny shores of distant islands, in the dazzling palaces of long-dead monarchs, or in the bustling streets of the world's capitals.

For families with children, the travel-centric library is a perfect place to whet their curiosity about the world. I urge parents to make up some photo albums with colorful covers, and photos in plastic sleeves, that the kids are encouraged to handle. Along with the "adult" furniture in the room, bring in a coffee table where you can put some photo albums that the kids can browse. Before long, I'm sure, you'll find them asking about the places you've been and things you've seen. It's a great way to begin sharing your travel stories.

## STEP INTO ANOTHER CENTURY

For avid readers of Dickens, for collectors of Victoriana, for men with nostalgia for an old-style club and women who wish they had Empire-style parlors, the home library is a perfect place to create the aura of a bygone era. Many kinds of images, decorations, and furnishings can create an atmosphere that will be conducive to reading and reflection. By grouping your collections or family ephemera together, you can truly create an impact. Here are a few objects that really lend that old-world charm:

» a favorite leather armchair with pillows, quilts, or throws

» a well-shaded floor lamp or table lamp, perfectly positioned for comfortable reading

» classic antique wooden bookcases bearing first-edition volumes, inherited sets of encyclopedias, family albums, series, or genealogies

» prints, etchings, daguerreotypes, and photos in genuine antique frames that establish the mood of the setting

OPPOSITE A softly lit library with classic paneling is the perfect location for highly valued photographs and paintings that are best preserved in a museum-like environment where they're protected from direct sunlight. ABOVE The cluster of portraits on the foyer table calls attention to the importance of family.

» heirloom collections of memorabilia, interspersed with the books on the shelves or placed on desk and tables

» reading and writing accoutrements—from ink-wells and fountain pens to classic quills

With antique furnishings, the worn grandeur of favorite book collections, and images of landscapes and family, the room itself becomes an archival work that can transport you into a completely different era.

# A STUDY FOR
# THE WHOLE FAMILY

**Once upon a time, the library—even a home library—was a place where you were supposed to talk in hushed tones, show absolute deference to studious readers, and make sure your entrances and exits were as discreet as possible. Then along came the twenty-first century. A lot has changed.**

Today, multitasking members of multigenerational households are drawn to a library that's a gathering place as well as a room for quiet contemplation. In many homes this is an area where kids and adults can hang out together, with TV, computer, and video games cheek-by-jowl with those antique reading devices called books and quaint writing implements like pen and paper. It's also a terrific place to bring out collectibles and reveal your interest in any kind of memorabilia. This room can become a staging area for anything that interests you—historically significant objects, crafts or artwork, entertainment, or sports.

The library shown here happens to be that of a man who, clearly, has a compelling interest in baseball memorabilia. A visitor to this room doesn't have to be sports crazed to appreciate the thematic elements all around. This is a wonderful example of the imaginative use of a library space as a display area as well as a convenient campground for kids and adults alike. All the memories are here—including volumes of baseball history held over from boyhood—but this theme has been playfully integrated into a welcoming space that is enjoyed by the whole family.

ABOVE For the shelves of his home library, this intrepid baseball fan has chosen dynamic porcelain figures and autographed baseballs to convey the history of his favorite sport.
OPPOSITE Though the staircase was imported from France, everything else in the library reflects one of America's greatest pastimes.

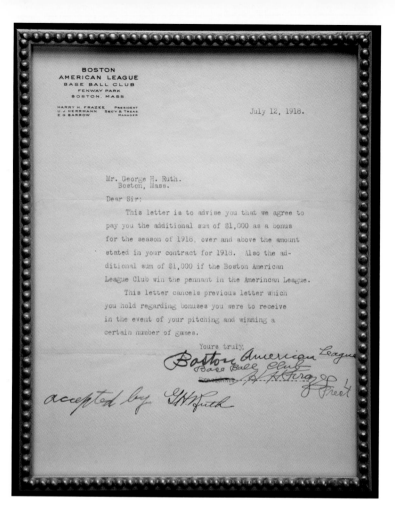

Of course, as soon as you see the statue of a ballplayer in the corner of the room, you know instantly that you're entering the library of a Red Sox fan. Then you are confronted with the very unusual sight of an old Red Sox sweater in a Plexiglas frame. As your eye travels about the room, you pick up on the many other indications of baseball lore—the small freestanding statue of a Red Sox player, bobble-headed baseball figurines on a shelf, signed baseballs in boxes. And you can see that there are kids in the family. Their photographs are on the shelves. A set of colored letters spells out "DAD" and next to it is a hand-lettered ceramic piece inscribed with the name of Dad's favorite team.

Not surprisingly, this ardent Red Sox fan grew up in Boston. By his own admission, he was "genetically coded," from birth, to give his heart and soul to this team. As a boy, he kept his transistor radio tuned in to the local sports station to pick up play-by-play announcements of the games, and when a double-header ran past his bedtime, he tucked the radio under his pillow to hear the final score.

The collection of baseball books started when his father brought home volumes from the Brattle bookstore, where he could get twenty for a dollar. The father noted his son's insatiable interest in baseball lore. Before long, the collection of baseball books had grown into the hundreds.

TOP Any doubt about Dad's priorities here? All the books are pushed back to give prime position to a favored bunch of miniature ballplayers alongside happy images of his own kids and their creations.

ABOVE In this example of a nineteenth-century technique known as "fore-edge book painting," the hand-painted baseball scene is only visible when the book is displayed in this fanned-out position.

LEFT Dressed in a historically accurate uniform, with proportions that are eerily lifelike, an iconic figure demands attention and boldly declares the theme of the room.

OPPOSITE Mirrors are a great way to add dimension and size to any room. Here, a fish-eye mirror is fun because it reflects all the colors in the collections and gives the impression of doubling the size of the room.

ABOVE The family's enjoyment of challenges and diversions spill over into this room with its books, art, games, and variety of collections, which all cohabit beautifully.

That interest has only increased over the years. Today, these carefully tended volumes purchased at bargain-basement prices—plus many more items of baseball memorabilia—occupy the paneled two-room library that was built expressly to house them. Though many books have been added, the ones with the greatest sentimental value are those saved from childhood.

Other baseball items that have come on board over the years include signed baseballs and attention-getting porcelain as well as bobble-head plastic figures of famous players. Best of all, for a baseball fanatic, is an original letter countersigned by Babe Ruth, agreeing to a bonus for his forthcoming year with the Red Sox.

Though the home is newly constructed (just nine years old at the time the photos were taken), the library itself appears as if it might have been built at the beginning of the previous century in another country. Its design was inspired by visits to National Trust estates in England. But despite the grandeur of the setting, the whole family now feels at home in Dad's Red Sox library. It is a place where the kids come to do their homework, play games, watch TV, or sit by the fire. It is very much a family room.

In fact, there is only one unfortunate aspect of this library created by a Red Sox supporter. Because of its proximity to New York, the boy in the family is growing up to be a Yankees fan.

# FAMILY
# PLACES

**W**hat's important to your family? What's important to you, personally? Easy questions to answer, perhaps, in your own mind, but if guests walked into your own home, would they be able to tell? There are many creative ways to integrate these personal and family items into your décor.

In this chapter I want to show you some homes where the values, history, and memories of family life aren't hidden away but are very much out in the open. In the homes shown here, memories surround the family in their daily lives. As you'll see, that doesn't mean the homes are crowded with dusty antiques or crammed with nostalgic photographs. On the contrary, in some homes, the memorabilia add just a touch—like a deft brushstroke—that the casual visitor may hardly notice at first. But if you visit more than once, you'll see more, and understand more, because the memories really are on display. They're just waiting to be discovered.

# DRINK AND EAT FROM YOUR HEIRLOOMS

Do you have family glassware, china, or silverware that's hidden away in a sideboard, cupboard, or closets for "special occasions"? Maybe the first of those special occasions is today, and another one is tomorrow. It isn't just a question of using what you have. It's a question of heritage.

If your tableware was inherited from your grandparents or great-grandparents, it holds many stories about how and where they lived and what was important to them. What celebrations occurred around the table that held this glass and china? How many times did your grandmother carefully wash and dry those dishes, shine the silver, and polish the glasses? The finger marks may be gone, but someone in your family chose those patterns and put food on these plates. They must have been handled with care to be so well preserved—and perhaps the person who passed them on to you had that very thought: "I want these to go to my children and grandchildren."

That doesn't mean they were meant to be museum pieces! In all likelihood, many have a story to tell. A bowl, even a beautiful bowl, is just a serving piece. But the bowl that a grandmother brought over from Ireland? Or the bowl that your aunt Teresa—who was such a wonderful cook—wanted you to have someday? That's quite a different story.

PREVIOUS PAGES Echoing all the motifs of home, kitchen, and garden, the tile work over the kitchen stove has an abundance of colorful images that are meaningful to every member of the household.

OPPOSITE You don't need to have complete matched sets of china or glassware; that's not what collecting is all about. As long as they're of a similar style and period—like this mixed assortment of cut-crystal goblets—they are perfect for everyday use.

ABOVE From chandelier to candelabra, glittering crystal sparkles throughout a room that, despite its glamour, is all about family.

# COMMISSIONING A PAINTED PORTRAIT

Much as I love the power of photography, a painted portrait conveys an elegance—even a grandeur—that may be exactly what you want in a family room. Portrait painting has a long and honored tradition. In the nineteenth century, nearly every gentleman of wealth would commission at least one portrait of himself and his family. Needless to say (as I'm sure you've noticed), the tradition continues to flourish today among politicians, corporate presidents, and benefactors.

A commissioned portrait is, indeed, a wonderful special tribute to the person you want to honor, but if it's going to work in your home, plan ahead and be selective about the artist you choose. Remember, you're looking not just for a good likeness but also for a work that has artistic merit and will fit in your environment.

Commissioning a portrait will involve some commitment of time as well as expense, so there are a few important considerations:

» *Make sure you know where it's going.* Unlike photographs, which we're likely to change over the years, a painted portrait usually has a permanent place in a room. It's advisable to decide the location beforehand, as its positioning will influence your decisions about the artist and style of the portraiture.

» *Pick a medium.* Do you prefer a portrait done in charcoal, watercolor, ink, oil, or some other medium? It's a matter of taste, but it's important to decide before you choose an artist.

» *Consider the size of the piece.* Decide on the dimensions in advance. The artist will need to know.

» *Look at the artist's previous work, and choose a style that appeals to you.* The portrait, of course, will be unique, but each artist has a distinctive style, and that's unlikely to change very much from one work to the next. Preferably get a preview of that work by visiting the artist's studio or gallery, viewing photographs of finished portraits, or visiting a website where the work is on display. You'll probably want to consider several different artists and get recommendations before making a final choice.

» *Ask how much time is involved.* Some artists will work only from life, and if you want an oil portrait, it may require several sittings, either in the studio or in your own home. This might be something to consider if you're an adult, but young children will have trouble sitting still. Often, artists do work from photographs, but might need a sitting before putting on the finishing touches.

ABOVE The area above the mantel is traditionally reserved for commissioned oils of storied ancestors, but in this twist, the children are featured.

# LIVING WITH
# YOUR MEMORIES

I love to see any kind of memorabilia—from family photographs to heirloom pieces—right in the middle of a place where there's a lot of family activity. For a great example, have a look at the music room shown above. It seems like everyone in this family loves to play some instrument, so

ABOVE Electric guitars, Victorian details, framed photos—these are the makings of a user-friendly music room where everyone in the family likes to spend time.

they spend a lot of time in this room. They could have made the choice to line the room with framed portraits of dead composers or posters of rock-star idols, but instead, the family put up many family photos. And they keep adding to the collection.

If you think about where your family spends a lot of time, consider how you can bring memories into that room. Typically, the living room becomes the more-or-less "designated area" where you'll find heirloom furniture or commissioned family portraits. And that's fine, of course. But what about all the time you spend in the kitchen? What about the TV room? The game room? The mudroom where everyone takes off their boots and hangs up their coats? All these are definitely living areas.

Why not bring your memories into the areas where you (and your spouse, and kids, and kids' friends, and friends of friends, and so on) really live? For many families, that place is the kitchen, and the focal point is the refrigerator door. Why? Because the kids are in and out of the kitchen all day, opening and closing the door of the fridge, so it's like a Happy Hallway on hinges. In my own home the refrigerator door is where I put snapshots of vacations and birthdays, newspaper clippings, announcements, and favorite sayings. Sometimes when I'm in the kitchen, I find myself getting nostalgic standing in front of the refrigerator remembering times that I've spent with family and friends. It's constantly evolving—just another way of showing that the family is important.

OPPOSITE The refrigerator door is not the only place to post photos, sayings, and messages. Anywhere in the house you can fill a wall, a corkboard, or a closet door with an entertaining and eye-catching assemblage of images and messages.
RIGHT An heirloom-in-the making, this inscribed silver photo album is permanently on display in the family homestead whose name it bears.

# PERSONALIZE THE FUTURE

In any shared living area, you forge the associations that will be shared by all the people you care about. That's why personalization is so important. I love to see a name, initial, or inscription on a piece in a family living area. I see it as a way of carrying forward.

If there's a letter opener, a cigarette case, or a silver compact with a set of initials on it, you can easily imagine a future relative wondering, someday, who owned that piece and what the initials stood for. And, with luck, someone will be able to tell the story.

Some people wonder whether these "personalized" items really do belong in everyday living areas. Shouldn't they be stowed away and preserved until the "right time"? In my view there's no better right time than right now. When you first bring personal items into public spaces, your kids or friends may have to guess at their meaning. They'll ask. You can tell. And in the telling, the history and heritage of your own life are created.

# FEED YOUR KIDS' CURIOSITY

I've noticed that many young kids seem to be less interested in their own parents than in distant generations. Often, old photographs are the first to get their attention.

I casually mix plenty of old family photographs with recent shots around my own home. The same can be done in more formal settings. A good example is the room shown opposite. This is a family of art lovers. The family spends a lot of time in a room that's hung with fine works (not for the kids), and the shelves and tables hold many superb art books. But right in the middle of the room, on a low coffee table where the children can sit and thumb through the pictures, are a number of photo albums I created for this family. And I'm told that the children automatically gravitate to those albums, open them up, and make their own discoveries. No monitoring required!

**ABOVE** Just because you have young children doesn't mean your home has to look like a preschool. Fill it with gallery-quality artwork that invites exploration and discovery.

LEFT With spiral-bound albums holding plastic-covered family photos, an elegantly appointed study welcomes the younger generation.

BELOW A low coffee table doubles as an adventure site, holding piles of art books alongside albums that are meant for small hands to explore.

# SHOWCASE YOUR FAMILY POSTCARDS

If you and your family members have traveled a lot over the years, you've probably collected postcards. It's a shame to keep them in storage, because they're such great conversation pieces, especially if you have children who might be intrigued by the stamps and postmarks and messages as well as the photographs. On the other hand, putting hundreds of postcards into albums is time-consuming work. So, what's the solution?

In my family room, on a table for anyone to see, displayed in an old leather box, are dozens of postcards that were sent to me by my mother and father when they traveled. My sister, Rina, and I always looked forward to getting these postcards when our parents were away. Now I can pick up one of those cards anytime, and it brings back a distinct childhood memory. One has a picture of a little Danish girl wearing a knee-length green skirt represented by a piece of cloth actually sewn onto the front of the card. On the other side it says, "Dear Monica, I just want you to have this doll from Denmark . . ." Another card has a view of Geneva. "All my love to the two best, prettiest,

most talented children in the world, and they are mine and their names are Monica and Rina. Had a half-hour stop in Geneva and sent you two cards from there." Signed "Love, your mommy," with three hand-drawn hearts.

Of course, these private messages were only meant for my sister and me to read. But now I like to leave them out where my own daughters can see them. And my daughters like getting this glimpse into their mother's past.

**RIGHT** This lovely reproduction Asian box, purchased nearly three decades ago, is the repository of treasured postcards from my parents.

# MIX THE ELEGANT WITH THE EVERYDAY

Why not have silver-framed portraits in your kitchen? Who says there are rules?

High-traffic areas may not seem like the obvious choice for beautiful frames and family photos, but why not? Mixing the artistic with the utilitarian is a fun way to help smooth the transition from the formal dining room to the casual kitchen.

Putting family photographs in silver frames creates a magnet for the eyes. Whatever you're doing in the kitchen—helping to cook, pouring a glass of juice, coming in to refill your coffee cup—I guar-

antee you won't be able to avoid being drawn to the portraits. It's the exceptional and playful incongruity of the display that gets your attention.

The contrast of bringing those "dining room" portraits into the kitchen works beautifully. If the display of photos is ever-changing, friends and family members always have something new to look at. Basically, this is a more elegant way of showcasing the same sentiments as the photo-covered fridge door with all its stickies, magnets, and slogans. Similar idea, but what a difference!

ABOVE In a dramatically cool, white-on-white eating area, images of infants and children, embracing and smiling, capture a story of family warmth.

# EXPRESS YOURSELF . . . TOTALLY

Whatever your passion may be—family, pets, art, music, theater, chess—express it fully throughout the décor of your home. Mimi Williams's Atlanta home is the uninhibited expression of her passionate interest in circles and circular sculpture.

Mimi is intrigued by the way circles represent infinity. No matter how many times you go around a circle, you will always wind up at the end, which is the same as the beginning, which is the same as the end. . . . And for as long as people have made drawings and left carvings on walls and created meaningful symbols, the circle has recurred as a universal art form. "Circles are a universal symbol of totality, wholeness, and original perfection," Mimi says. "Roundness is the most natural and sacred shape."

To Mimi the circle is a symbol that communicates many messages. It is the feminine force in nature. It also represents spacelessness (because it has no above or below). It recurs throughout nature—in solar cycles, for instance—and for these and many other reasons, the circle has become linked to numerous spiritual rituals and deities.

Obviously Mimi's connection to circles and their meaning is very personal, enforced by her beliefs about culture, symbolism, and the expression of philosophy through imagery. What's unusual in her home is the way she has brought that fascination out into the open. This collection is Mimi's expression of her inner life and also something that she wants to share with her family and with anyone who comes into her home.

What fascinates me is how much this room expresses her own passionate interests. She's constantly adding to this display, using what she finds in her travels and research.

This is a far cry from hanging up a family picture, but just as expressive in communicating emotional and spiritual life and sharing it with your family and friends.

ABOVE From the conversation area in Mimi's living room, every guest has a view of the sculpture and found objects that echo and repeat her single most-favorite theme.

FAMILY PLACES | 77

TOP For dog lovers, here's the ultimate collection—canine-shaped doorstops rescued from antiques stores and flea markets.
ABOVE In what is clearly a sign of respect, these expressive images of a much-loved pet are elegantly framed and displayed.
RIGHT Poised on the top of an antique desk, in the familiar stance, one small figure of a guard dog assumes large-scale proportions in this setting.

ABOVE "Dallas Among the Flowers," a gift from a watercolor artist, was a portrait of a beloved setter who was actually named "Alice." After Alice passed away, the owners took a hint from the artist and decided their next setter would indeed be named "Dallas."

LEFT The framed painting—now considered a tribute to both Alice and Dallas—has pride of place in a casual breakfast nook.

# HONOR YOUR PETS

When you see a dog's portrait in a family living area, you know at once this is an important friend who is very much part of the household. In my clients' homes I've seen painted portraits, sketches, and photographs of dogs, cats, birds, and horses that everyone in the family knows by name. The message can't be missed: these animals are much loved. Here are some ways to include them:

» Treat pet portraiture like family portraiture. If you commission single portraits of your family members, be sure to include your pets, either alone or with family members.

» Have your kids create pictures of your pets and display them. They can write the name of the pet right on the drawing.

» Create a collection around a breed. Many breeds are depicted in paintings, on pottery and china, in tapestry and embroidery work, and on household items.

» Look for first-class photos. Photographers such as William Wegman, Bruce Weber, and many others use dogs in their artistic photography. You can tell these photographers have a great rapport with their "models," and the fine photographs, in addition to being artistic work, have huge appeal for dog lovers. Pet owners as well as art lovers can enjoy these classic images. If you're a collector of such photos, put them on display.

## GET COMFORTABLE WITH YOUR HEIRLOOMS

What do you do when you inherit your grandmother's piano and couch? Do you put them on display like a museum piece, or do you live with them?

I'm always happy to see everyone in the household treat family heirlooms like any other piece of furniture. What could be a picture of greater contentment than the one opposite, with family pets making themselves at home on an antique sofa that used to sit in Grandma's living room. That's a good example of a family who gets comfortable with their heirlooms and makes them part of everyday life. In the same room there's a small spinet piano (above). It's an heirloom piece that might get heaps of commendation on *Antiques Roadshow*, but instead of being cordoned off and revered like a museum piece, it's actually used by family members.

Heirlooms may be rare and valuable, but they weren't meant to be treated as relics. Sometimes, casual inclusiveness is the best way to show respect.

OPPOSITE Though an antique of immeasurable value, Grandma's old spinet is just a practice piano to the kids in the family.
ABOVE There's no question about who has first dibs on the most cozy heirloom in the house.

# CREATE A
# FOCAL POINT

Not long ago, I was commissioned to do some photographs for a family with a big loft in Manhattan. I was intrigued to see how they'd taken small, important objects from their family collection and given them a stature that transcends their actual size. Their loft is a bare open space with a vast expanse of flooring. At the far end of the room, light pours in through huge, uncurtained windows. This is the room where the family spends most of their time. It's living room, family room, recreation room, and library all in one.

Arrayed on the ledges in front of those windows is the wonderful collection of iconic-looking figurines. Alongside are pieces that the family picked up in their travels and some of the children's artwork. On the brightly lit sill, the effect is almost ethereal. The pieces come from the family's far-flung travels to Africa, Russia, Japan, and the Middle East. But the wonderful creations made by the kids mingled among the gifts and artifacts are just as important.

What would this space be without this collection as a focal point? The collection ties in beautifully the family's love of travel with the children's gifts of expression. The presence of the small figures and sculptures warms the room. Placed as they are, and backlit by natural light, they're a larger-than-life presence. And they also create a satisfying link to the world beyond. Outside the windows stand apartment buildings and skyscrapers; inside, seen from this family's perspective, the objects on the shelf seem to rival those buildings in size and scale. In terms of their personal significance to the family, they stand tallest of all.

OPPOSITE **Poised in the foreground in this loft apartment, calm statues of Buddha pervade the space with an aura of contentment.**

TOP **I helped this family solve the problem of what to hang on a curved wall—small photos in large box frames that add a sculptural dimension.**

ABOVE **A daughter's handcrafted vase and a painting done by her mother at the same age are just as important in this home as the century-old artifacts collected in their travels.**

# WHERE THE HOME
# SAYS WHO WE ARE

**In some homes, serendipity is the style that helps to create a legacy and preserve a heritage. With the right sensibility, the memorabilia assembled in a home may seem arbitrary, but it all has meaning to the family.**

**Some years ago, when I was commissioned to photograph some young children in the home of Cory and Bill, I was struck by a number of details around their home that seemed to have special significance. It wasn't until later that I began to understand the family's emotional investment in their collections. Nearly every room in the house displayed evidence of the family's self-expression.**

Coming into the kitchen, for instance, you would immediately notice the number of pieces of antique porcelain with vivid cobalt blue patterns. It all began with a single pitcher that was an engagement present from Bill to Cory, and for her the inspiration for what is now an extensive collection of antique stoneware.

Cory's love of the blue stoneware has taken her on a quixotic search from antiques stores and flea markets to Internet sites. Over the years, the collection has grown to include bowls, jugs, pitchers, and vases, all with distinctive and elaborate blue designs.

In the same kitchen, your gaze will be drawn inexorably to the colorful tile behind the stove with

RIGHT Each piece of blue stoneware is unique in design and function, but when grouped together, they make a single statement.

OPPOSITE Embraced by the spiraling balustrade in a formal entryway, a round table with family vacation pictures greets the visitor.

ABOVE Framed by identical cabinetry, two impressive sets of pottery take on the quality of yin and yang, contrasting the earth tones of one collection with the lighter-hued whites and blues of another.

OPPOSITE A whole collection—like the "William" cups shown here—can be built around a name, an initial, or a thematic link like style, color, or historical period. It's up to you to decide what's the unifying theme.

its extraordinary array of homespun imagery. Portrayed in the tile work is a quirky assortment of images that have personal appeal to each member of the family. In brushwork there's the painting of a horse in a paddock, an affirmation of the family's love of the outdoors. In the foreground is a picture of one of the family dogs. For each member of the family, there is an image that has a particular meaning. Pepsi, the wife's favorite drink, is included. The blue stoneware around the kitchen shows up again—two dimensionally—in the painting behind the stove. All the family's favorite things have been gathered up and respectfully

portrayed in a single mural in the most-frequented part of the house.

But the kitchen is only the beginning. Other motifs, and reminders of family connections, inhabit every room. For son William, the family has sought cups imprinted with his name. It's been a successful search, as you can see from the photo opposite. Additions to the "William cup" collection are always welcome, and everyone (friends as well as family) is on the lookout for new additions. And of course there's no question that William will one day inherit the many cups and mugs that bear his name.

# 4

# PERSONAL
# SPACES

According to Marcel Proust's housekeeper, Celeste Albaret, her reflective employer was fanatically precise about what was and was not to be in the bedroom, where he did all his writing. Celeste describes "his three tables, arranged within arm's reach," the old bedside table that held "manuscripts, notebooks, a schoolboy inkwell, penholder, a watch, a bedside lamp," and the third walnut table for his coffee tray and his lime and pitcher of Evian water. "And all this was very simple," she concludes, "like a little island in that vast room amid all that massive furniture."

In our homes, we all have "little islands," personal spaces where we spend some of our most satisfying hours, in an environment (tidy or not!) that is entirely our own. These little islands are perfect places where we can live with our Proustian recollections and also the places where we can work, play, reflect, or dream.

How you go about creating and furnishing your little island will depend, of course, very much on the size of your home and the makeup of your household. If your personal space is limited, your island might be no bigger than a desk, dressing table, or nightstand. In a bigger home, perhaps you have an entire room you can call your own. But however much area you have, this is a very important part of the house.

In this chapter you'll see some of the private spaces that have caught my attention. I'm sure you already have an "island" in your home, but I hope this will give you further ideas about personalizing the space that you call your own.

## MAKE YOUR BEDROOM MORE LIVABLE

For some people, a bedroom is just a place where the bed is. For others, however, it's much more: A place for resting and reading. A place where you surround yourself with favorite collectibles. Where you spend time reading and writing letters to friends.

The desk shown on page 78 is part of a bedroom that has been furnished with collectibles that create a totally personalized living area. This personal space has been turned into a room that's also a library, a study, and a display area. In the same bedroom is the unique collection of painted-iron dog-shaped doorstops, also shown on page 78.

In the bedroom shown opposite, a dressing-table mirror becomes a frame for scores of photographs. You can see how, by placing a melange of family photographs around the frame of a dressing-table mirror, you can begin every day surrounded by a

sea of good memories. There need not be any logic in the arrangement; feel free to place photographs willy-nilly. The important thing is that the display be exuberant.

PREVIOUS PAGES A utilitarian bathroom shelf has been transformed into a display area for jewelry and memorabilia.

ABOVE This little glass table was a "find" in an antiques store, perfect for holding a small collection of perfume bottles.

RIGHT Like benign observers of a daily ritual, images of family and friends are tucked around the entire perimeter of a dressing-room mirror.

all
of
his
steps
led
only
to
her
door

OPPOSITE A bedside table is a great place for a personal collection like this small group of objects in Nicky Hilton's Bel Air bedroom. ABOVE Unlike the desks of another era that needed to hold an array of writing instruments, Nicky's desk with its slim laptop has a chic simplicity.

## GATHER SOME THINGS IN YOUR BATHROOM

One of the most-visited rooms in the house some-times gets neglected when it comes to finding a place for heirlooms, photographs, and collectibles. There are many creative ways to use the walls, shelves, and counters of a bathroom. In my own bathroom, I've created a display area for a collection featuring some pottery in a wonderful, serene celadon. The collection began with just one or two celadon jars. Later, I added celadon-colored ware

from antiques stores and flea markets. I was delighted when one of my daughters, in an art-class project, made some pottery that was the same color. When the pottery came home from school, I added those pieces to the display.

In a bathroom that doubles as a dressing room, there are many ways to make personal items part of the décor, especially those that are most impor-tant to you. The first time I visited BJ's home, I was delighted with what I discovered in her bathroom. On the shelf—in full display—she had created a personal space filled with her huge collection of jewelry. Clearly, she loved having these things at hand so she could casually put on one piece of

OPPOSITE A cluster of children's portraits greets their parents when they enter the dressing area of their bathroom.
ABOVE Original photographs over the tub are well sealed in heavy frames, but even so, any originals should be replaced every few months to avoid being damaged by moisture.
LEFT One of my favorite pottery collections sits on wall-mounted molding in my bathroom. It mingles the school projects of my children with vintage pieces in a way that says all are equally important to me.

jewelry or take off another at a moment's notice. And it wasn't just jewelry. BJ's charm bracelet hangs over the edge of a restaurant guest check that's been carefully placed in a picture frame. When BJ, as a teenager, worked as a waitress in Key West, she regularly waited on Tennessee Williams and his various companions. She figured his guest check was a memento worth saving. Now it occupies a place of honor on her bathroom shelf—a receipt for broiled snapper for two, $17.70, dou-

bling as a hanger for the charm bracelet that she kept from childhood.

You can also bring photographs into the bathroom and display them the way they are shown above and opposite. One word of warning, however: You should anticipate that moisture is going to get to the photographs and do some damage after a while. This is not a room for archive-quality or irreplaceable photos.

# EXPRESS YOUR PASSIONS

As you can see from the examples on these pages, there are inventive and whimsical ways to make entire rooms or parts of your home uniquely your own. Be open to the many ways in which your passions and interests can be expressed. For some people, that means photographs—lots of them. But others love to collect ceramics, lamps, gift items, prints, and many other kinds of collectibles. Having been in so many homes, I made a very precise count of the number of ways people choose to express themselves in their private spaces. That number is one gazillion.

LEFT A dedicated horse lover devotes a corner of her bedroom to photographs, sculptures, and books about her favorite animal.
ABOVE Elsewhere in the bedroom, finely sculpted solid-brass bookends repeat the equestrian theme.

Often, the place can be quite small. And the cherished object is unaccompanied. But it always remains in its place. It could be a note from a spouse, a friend, or a loved one. A piece of jewelry that brings back wonderful memories. Or something that was made for you. It's nice to have one little space where such things belong.

Sometimes you can take a very mundane space and make it fun. At right is a well-designed hideaway that truly belongs to the man of the house. In an area that might have been totally dedicated to shirt storage, he has turned his private space into something more than a well-appointed gentleman's dressing room. On the dresser top is an intimate collection of snapshots and his children's artwork. In an ovoid stone bowl nestles a collection of

OPPOSITE The cabinet doors were expressly equipped with crisscrossed elastic ribbons holding all sizes of favorite photos or snapshots. No tape or tacks needed!

ABOVE One gentleman's wood-framed dressing area resembles a small-scale haberdashery, with a counter holding cards, photos, and memorabilia that are unmistakably personal.

LEFT Among the special items on that counter—a bowl lined with a collection of the heart-shaped stones that his wife has given to him over the years.

beautiful polished hearts made of glass, stone, and porcelain. These are gifts from his wife, who collects various kinds of heart-shaped stones wherever she travels, then gives them to friends and family as gifts.

In the bedroom shown here, a whole flock of necklaces has escaped the confines of their jewelry boxes. All around the books and shelves are scores of necklaces of every conceivable shape and size, strung with beads of stones, ceramics, shells, and even some precious stones. These are inherited pieces. Every necklace has a story and a special meaning. Clearly, this is someone who values every one of her favorite adornments and enjoys seeing them out in the open as opposed to having them locked in a drawer or closet. The art of choosing which she's going to wear, and when, is a luxurious and satisfying daily ritual.

OPPOSITE AND ABOVE It never occurred to the owner of these necklaces to hide her treasures in drawers and cases. Instead, she used nails and hooks to put her entire collection on permanent display.

# CHARMS ARE FOREVER

Many women who were given charm bracelets when they were young girls still have them tucked away somewhere, and can even remember who gave them each trinket and talisman on the chain. Charm bracelets probably reached the height of popularity in the mid-1950s, but their history goes back much further. From Neolithic times, there's evidence that people carried special smooth stones or pieces of wood—primitive "charms"—to ward off enemies. Domestic trinkets came to be regarded as lucky charms, valued for bringing good fortune and driving away evil spirits. During the age of the pharaohs, Egyptian women wore wrist and neck bracelets with special charms that were meant to adorn them in the afterlife. Knights of the Middle Ages carried charms and amulets to bring them luck in their crusading ventures.

The charm bracelet became a hugely popular item of decorative fashion jewelry for Queen Victoria. The women of her time took note and strove to emulate her. By the early twentieth century, the "charms" that had once been empowered to bring good luck and drive away evil spirits had turned into a fashion statement.

The charm bracelets that many of us created are only distantly related to previous incarnations. But as conjuring devices, they still work well, given their power to remind us of important occasions, romantic relationships, and almost-magical moments. Each charm has a special meaning, depending on who gave it to us (a best friend, a boyfriend, a parent) or the occasion when it was given (graduation, birthday, wedding). These are more than trinkets. Added over the years, sometimes saved from early childhood or teenage years, charm bracelets are indeed a charming reminder of where we've been, whom we've known, and what we've done in our lives.

I encourage women to take out their charm bracelets and wear them. Jackie Onassis, Pearl Bailey, and the Duchess of Windsor—among many other trendsetters—all wore beautiful charm bracelets. The charms tell a story of special days and times and friends. If the chain you had as a teenager still fits, wear it and keep adding to it. Or transfer charms from an old bracelet to a new one. The time will come when you'll want to pass it along to a daughter, niece, or a young friend.

OPPOSITE Displayed on an heirloom brass stand and draped over gilded vintage frames, the charms and pendants in this collection are meant to be admired for their associations and remembrances as well as their value as jewelry.

# FILL UP A BOARD

Wherever you "set up shop" in your home, a small bulletin board helps create an instant personal space. One of my favorite variations is the French memo board, like the one shown here in the home of designer Alex Papachristidis. Ribbons criss-cross a fabric background to hold reminders, memos, invitations, and notes interspersed with photographs. It's easy to add or remove notes or photographs that are tucked under the ribbon. The French board becomes an expression of social and family life and also keeps a dynamic record of activities and memories you'd like to hold on to.

Corkboards and bulletin boards are great as well, and they come in many shapes and sizes. You can purchase a low-cost bulletin board at any

office supply store, then wrap the plain wood edges with a colorful fabric or patterned paper to create an attractive display area. Hang up the board, or just lean it against the wall, and begin to fill it with your favorite messages, sayings, photographs, and clippings.

Cork is also obtainable in sheets, like wallpaper, that can be glued onto the wall. The advantage of this wall covering is that it's unframed, so you can expand it in any direction.

And don't forget the refrigerator door! Whether or not that door was ever intended to be a display area, magnets have made anything possible. In my own home, as I've mentioned, it's a favorite location for recent postings.

OPPOSITE A French board mounted on a desk is the perfect backdrop for an inveterate letter writer. ABOVE With vintage Gucci frames establishing red as the theme, similar tones were introduced to the valance, curtains, and other features of the room.

# REMIND YOURSELF OF YOUR FAVORITE PEOPLE

Throughout your house there are many places where you can plant reminders of special moments. One of my friends has three of her children's paintings that she carefully framed and placed in an upstairs hallway near their rooms. The paintings, signed by her daughters, are bold and colorful. But to her they are more than cute artwork. That little cluster of pictures is a reminder of one rainy day in 1993 when all of her daughters sat at a single table, painting their favorite flowers. Every time she passes by those paintings, she remembers three little girls and a rainy afternoon.

In my own personal space, I have some lockets, compacts, boxes, and cases that I fill with photos and keep shut. Anyone can open the lockets and cases and look inside, but for me, each photograph has a personal meaning because it is of someone who has been a big part of my life. In my clients' homes, I encourage them to bring their personalized items into the open: A vintage silver case, for instance, that has a meaningful engraving. A closed photo case with "Happy Birthday" on the cover. An old locket on a ribbon that hangs from a hook, a knob, or the edge of a picture frame. I know that the picture, the message, or the engraving has special meaning for the person who keeps these items nearby. Those reminders of friends and family are very much a part of their own lives, and though I may look, I realize I am just a visitor, while, for them, the significance of the image or message is deeply personal.

Sometimes, the space that you call your own can be literally as small as a single tray. Like a canvas waiting to be painted on, that tray is a blank slate that you can fill with favorite portraits and photographs of the people who are most important to you. Place it on a side table, keep it in the kitchen, or move it to your bedroom. Wherever the tray travels, the warm memories go with it.

OPPOSITE Converted from photo to fabric through a screening process, images are sewn onto a single pillow.
ABOVE While most families choose to put photos on side tables, in this sparsely appointed bedroom the attention-getting pillow with family photos is the first thing you see when you come in the room.
RIGHT Three young children created these works of art on a rainy weekend. Years later, their mother framed their work, painted a wall with a complementary color, and made her children's art a permanent decorative element in the home.

# INSCRIBE NOW

Whenever I see a name or set of initials on a watch, a piece of jewelry, a picture frame, or a personal accessory, it makes me think how meaningful this could be to someone in the future. Names and initials are more than a form of identification or personal vanity, as anyone who has inherited an inscribed heirloom will tell you. As soon as something is inscribed, the memories attached to it will live forever.

You don't need to limit yourself to names and initials, either. When you're trying to create new heirlooms that are part of your life—and for your family in the future—let it be about you. Do you have a passion for chocolate? You can engrave the name of your favorite chocolate. If you love to dance, have the image of a dancer inside a locket or cigarette case. Or enclose your favorite philosophical quote, a line of a poem, or a mantra.

**LEFT** In a sentimental grouping, a couple's wedding photo, anniversary book, and birthday memorabilia are ever-present reminders of significant events. In any family, heirloom-quality silver is sure to be passed along from one generation to the next.

**ABOVE** Each silver hairbrush is a faithful reproduction of a vintage design, but engraved initials add a personal touch.

**OPPOSITE** Trays, trays, trays—when colorful boxes are displayed like this, they become a more important grouping.

# INDULGE YOUR BLISS

**Everyone needs an area in their home where they can find respite and enjoy what they truly love to do. Even if you don't have a whole room that you can call your own, it's important to carve out a space for yourself. The content of that space is more important than the size of it. In a corner of a room, for instance, you can create your sewing area, or painting area, or writing area, if you just "move in," put things in place, and let the other members of your household know that this area is not to be disturbed. Once that zone is established, you may be surprised how it's respected.**

Of course, in the best of all possible worlds, most of us would love to have a whole room (at least!) designated as a special place, all to ourselves, where we can pursue our most passionate interests. For Josie Natori, the dream of such a place has been turned into a reality. As a little girl growing up in the Philippines, Josefina Almeda Cruz was the oldest of six children. She started to play piano when she was just four years old. She loved the instrument, had extraordinary natural ability, and with the kind of dedication unusual for a child of her age, her talent blossomed. At the age of nine, she gave her first concert performance with the Manila Philharmonic Orchestra. Though her passion for music did not wane, young Josie felt that she had a better future in business than in the arts, and eight years after that concert, at age seventeen, she left Manila for New York, where she studied economics at Manhattanville College. That led to her launching a stellar career in finance and, later, founding the company that she heads today.

During her years in business, her love of music never faded. "A piano has always been the first thing I have in a home," says Josie. After graduating from college and moving into her own apartment, her first purchase was a Steinway. For her

ABOVE Precious items on a dressing table—in a single box containing scents, heirloom pieces, and a candle—help start the day.
OPPOSITE For someone who loves her shoes and accessories, rows of open shelves are far more appropriate than secret hiding places behind closed closet doors.

fiftieth birthday—forty-one years after her first performance in the Philippines—Josie gave a concert in Carnegie Hall.

Josie arranged to have her own concert grand piano moved to the hall for her performance. Afterward, the piano was transported to her home and hoisted by crane to the level of her music room. Today she calls that private space "my favorite room in the entire house."

At least once a week, Josie and her music coach play concerts together in this room. While she may never again perform in Carnegie Hall, the memory is always here—in the most tangible form—every time she sits down to play. It's a far different place than the living room in Manila where four-year-old Josie tapped out her first scale on an old upright. But every time Josie enters her music room, the memories of all her hours at the piano fill the room along with the strains of Schumann, Chopin, Rachmaninoff, Brahms, and Liszt.

OPPOSITE Josie Natori's music room is elegant and spare, serving as a private haven for practicing and enjoying music.

ABOVE With doors removed and tiny pedestals installed, a closet was transformed into a display cabinet for an incomparable collection of ancient figurines.

LEFT An enduring record of myriad hours enjoyed at the piano, well-thumbed music books are like a personal history of many years of practicing and performing.

# 5

# STAIRCASES TO
# REMEMBER

**H**ow long does it take to walk up a flight of stairs?

In most homes, climbing at a leisurely pace, ten seconds? Less?

Then imagine a staircase that might take ten *minutes* . . . or twenty . . . or thirty . . . to climb. And imagine that every step of the way, you are distracted or preoccupied by the photographs displayed on the wall taking you on a tour of a child and her family—almost from the moment she was born to nearly the present day.

A staircase like that is more than a transitional space from one floor to the next. It's a time machine. On each step you can visit a moment that captures an image from the past. You can spend as much time with that image as you like before you take another step up or down—into the next month or year of a person's life, or one step deeper into their past.

PREVIOUS PAGES If pets are important family members, their portraits deserve a special place in your home, like this stairway "gallery" where color photographs are on display.

ABOVE Leading from door to stairway, mirrors in assorted frames tempt each visitor to look again and again before ascending.

Any home with a staircase offers the ultimate gallery space, and the only question is how you'd like to use it. I've visited many homes where a stairway captures multiple generations, and the stories they tell are fascinating. Take a step up or down, and there may be photographs introducing the visitor to relatives from the even-more-distant past; pictures of children who are adults today; as well as views of family homes, holidays, and cele-

brations. On staircases with multigenerational displays, where time stands still, you will usually need a knowledgeable guide to make sense of it all. Ideally, there's one family member who has fabulous recall of faces, chronology, events, and family history—who can identify nearly every participant by sight and association and place them in the context of current generations. Otherwise, as a visitor to the family stairway, you may find yourself entirely on your own trying to figure out—as you mount the stairway step by step—how all the characters are connected in this family-centric gallery.

I also find that families take varying attitudes toward transitions as well as traditions on these stairways. Some seem to designate a permanent place for each of the pictures—never to be disturbed as long as the homestead is intact—while others use their multileveled gallery for temporary display of an ever-changing heritage exhibit of lives in transition.

Here are some ideas of what you can do.

# MIX YOUR PRINTS, PAINTINGS, AND PHOTOS

A staircase is the ideal place for what is essentially a multimedia display, because the viewer is constantly moving (either up stairs or down!). You can create a vast amount of interest by mixing different styles and historical periods that become fertile territory for storytelling. You can set the stage for these photos by selecting a wallpaper that's right. In the stairway shown here, for instance, the family chose a wallpaper that's a serene shade of blue, with a traditional pattern that conveys a strong sense of history.

In a wide, spacious staircase, you might choose to have a collection of photographs that are in identical frames and hung gallery-style. But more often, the family staircase begs for variety, and if you have charcoal drawings, even newspaper clippings and photographs, it's easy to piece together an arrangement that makes for easy viewing.

TOP Highlighting precious Meissen pottery inherited from grandparents, the woman who acquired the pieces has placed them in front of a large oval mirror outside her bedroom, where their reflection makes them look even grander.

ABOVE At the second-floor landing, the guardrail establishes a visual horizontal axis, adding a bold underline to the array of portraits.

# HAVE FUN WITH YOUR CLUTTER

One of my favorite staircases is the one shown here. It looks as if the family emptied every box and drawer to reveal the delightful hodgepodge of family life. Within some very large frames are gathered multiple snapshots of truly memorable or nearly forgotten events—the awarding of a soccer trophy, Boy Scout trips, family vacations, birthdays, anniversaries, all sorts of family gatherings dating from decades ago to just last year. Here and there are single framed portrait photos, but most of the comfortable clutter is displayed in vertical and horizontal rows within a great variety of oversize frames that seem barely able to contain everything that's happened to this active and colorful family. Best of all, the clutter effect is a complete contrast to the very elegant and classic lines of a nineteenth-century staircase designed by the famed architect Stanford White, with a banister that has been impeccably restored. To see a collection like that across from handcrafted railings and beautifully polished finials is like having a household of irreverent kids turned loose in a Victorian parlor.

RIGHT The elegant staircase was designed by famed architect Stanford White, but everything else in this stairway says home and family, with walls that are jam-packed with an assortment of framed pictures of sports events, school occasions, and other memorable moments.

# BE STAGEY

At the opposite end of the design spectrum, a staircase can also be used as a dramatic showcase for single works of art or a sequence of large portraits. Working with large pieces, of course, requires more planning and allows less flexibility than a staircase collection comprised of smaller images. But on the right kind of staircase—particularly one that can be viewed from a wide-open lower hallway or an upper gallery—the "stage effect" can be truly dramatic.

In this Beverly Hills home, the family decided they wanted a gridlike display all around the landing at the top of the stairway. All the frames are exactly the same. Architecturally, it's a very clean look, but the Spartan design only draws further attention to the photographs themselves. Since the frames are all alike, any viewer will tend to concentrate on the images. Everything is in keeping with the modern décor, but the display of photographs makes the whole space inviting.

RIGHT With sunlight pouring in from an overhead skylight and clerestories, it was essential to use UV-protective glass to preserve this series of art-quality family photographs.

ABOVE An art lover's aerie on a high landing provides an incomparable vista of a virtual alleyway of archive-quality photographs, prints, and etchings.

OPPOSITE When surrounding yourself with things you love, you don't have to favor a single style. Here, much of the art and furniture is contemporary, while objects mounted on books and sideboards include pieces collected in many years of travel.

# MEMORIES
# ON MANY LEVELS

In the Manhattan town house shown here, the family specifically designed the living areas of their home for modern art. The space where they display their art collection is open and expansive. But there's one area of the home—a stairway leading from one display area to the next—where a visitor feels embraced by the warmth of the family.

All along the wall of that stairway, space has been set aside for an array of intimate, important, and very personal family photographs. Some of those photographs were taken by family members, but many were selected from photographs of their daughter that I've been taking almost since the day she was born.

As this is a family of art lovers, their selection naturally involves some aesthetic decisions regarding selection and placement. But one of the things I love about their "memory stairway" is that it's not a static, formal arrangement. The images on this stairway create a very special private place within an otherwise expansive and boldly designed home. This one staircase will always be for family.

Though much of the focus is on the daughter, cousins, siblings, and others are also remembered—and honored—in this space. Near the top of the stairs is a photograph of the girl and her grandmother crouched over a table as they solve a crossword puzzle together. The grandmother has since passed away, and the crossword puzzle they finished together has been lost. But great memories live on in this photograph.

RIGHT Taking advantage of a two-story window with a multistory view, a well-lit contemplative reading area has been created next to the home library.
OPPOSITE A staircase is a perfect tableau for displaying many cherished family photographs. The tight collage makes for a pleasing mosaic effect.

ABOVE Single works of art—unlike thematic collections—can be placed anywhere in a house or an apartment to be viewed in isolation as individual works. In the town house shown here, the largest pieces are in the living room, but many other contemporary paintings and sculptures are placed throughout bedrooms and hallways.

ABOVE Ceramic pieces mounted on Plexiglas easels are the creations of a child, holding their own among paintings and sculpture from mature artists. In this home, clearly both sets of work have equal importance.

Many photographs of the daughter were taken on the spur of the moment. The day she lost her first tooth, I got a call from her mother and took the photo that now hangs near the bottom of the staircase. The day the daughter adopted a puppy, I got another call and caught some of the earliest moments of their jubilant meeting. And there are many more images as well—playful moments with stuffed animals, pets, and toys. When her mother came back from a trip to South America with a collection of hats, her daughter transformed herself from Spanish dancer (in a gaudy wide-brimmed sombrero) to mellow-toned gentle woman (in a striking bowler-style hat). Both photos are on the staircase.

From the year when she took care of a friendly guinea pig, there's a photograph of a proud little girl with a cavy on her head. Another year, a drama unfolded when she got into a costume box, coming up with an immense boa that she strung around her neck and the outfit of a prima ballerina.

On the staircase shown on page 125, each photo seems to tell a story, and some have backstories. This girl has a photo of her father as a child, standing on his head. For his birthday, she wanted to give him a portrait of herself standing on *her* head. Now both generations of head standers are side by side on the staircase wall.

In other parts of the house—in the bedrooms and the library—are family snapshots taken when the family went on trips or gathered for special occasions. But the stairway is the centerpiece, and its purpose never changes. As long as the family lives in this town house, the stairway will be a constant reminder of a child growing up in a loving family.

# HOW TO PHOTOGRAPH CHILDREN: SOME GUIDELINES

In family life, I'm sure there have been many times when you've said to yourself, "I wish I had a picture of that." These are moments that cannot be planned or prepared for. And it's one of the reasons I recommend you always have a camera at hand. Today, that's easier than ever to do.

When I first began taking photographs, I used a single-lens reflex (SLR) camera with black-and-white film. I still use a 35-mm film camera and love what I can do with black-and-white film, so I haven't changed my preferences. You really have infinite choice among cameras, but the photographic equipment does not entirely determine the quality of your photographs. Capturing an important family moment has less to do with technology than with *seeing*.

Here are what I consider essential guidelines for shooting photographs of children.

## DON'T BOTHER WITH POSING

It's okay for kids to pose at first, but that's only a beginning. If you want to see kids doing what they do naturally, they have to be on the move— playing, searching, straying, staring, or jumping rope. If you want the best moments, you need to catch kids when they're swinging on swings, jumping off chairs, exploring a garden, looking for lost pets, taking time-outs, peeking through a fence, or reaching into a sink to wash their hands.

## BE ACTIVE

If the children are deep in activity, that means you have to be active as a photographer, too. You can't stay in one place and hope that the action will come to you. When you're photographing children, follow them around, ask what they're interested in, and find out what they're doing.

## GET DOWN TO THEIR LEVEL

Do you know what the world looks like to a child who is three and a half feet tall? This is the way to find out. Crouch down with your camera. Have a seat on the grass. If a child is peeking through a fence to see what's on the other side, get down to the same level and right behind her. That's where you'll get the best shot.

## LET THEM DRESS DOWN

There's no point "dressing up" girls in crinoline and lace or putting boys in their best suits. When you do that, too often their behavior changes to match their outfits. That's not what you want as a photographer. They won't feel comfortable, and they certainly won't act natural. Sometimes when I arrive at a house, I find everyone dressed up for the occasion. While I might take some shots of them in their dress-up clothes, I know I won't discover what these kids are all about until they go ahead and change into something else.

## CATCH THEM IN THE MOMENT *AFTER* THE MOMENT

Every parent wants to capture the instant when Beth or Billy blows out the candles on the birthday cake. That moment will be lost forever if we don't catch it. So go ahead—shoot that scene—but don't put your camera away yet. The best shot may be coming up in the "moment after the moment"—when one of the young guests sticks her finger in the cake or your child starts playing with a ribbon, or Aunt Sally ladles out the ice cream. Keep shooting.

## TAKE *LOTS* OF PICTURES

With digital cameras, you can get dozens of images, download them, view them, and discard the throwaways without worrying about film processing. But even if you're using regular film, the "waste" may seem like a lot at first, but it really isn't waste at all. A professional photographer always shoots a lot of film, knowing the more pictures we take, the better our chances of getting just the right moment. It's not unusual to shoot ten rolls—360 images—and get only a few great shots. (Of course, you might get a lot more.)

## KEEP YOUR CAMERA OUT AT ALL TIMES

A photograph has the power to capture a single moment—just one instant, frozen in time. But if you want to record that instant, you need to have your camera ready!

If you're in the kitchen, have your camera on the shelf. When you're traveling, keep it in your pocket or purse. Don't ask your kids to pose or smile. Just shoot. You never know when the moment will be right, but as long as your camera is nearby, you can use it anytime. If you see the right moment, then have to go somewhere to retrieve your camera, by the time you get back, the moment may be lost.

## REMEMBER, THERE'S NO "BAD STAGE"

Some parents stop taking pictures when their kids go through an awkward stage, like getting braces. My philosophy is, Why stop taking pictures? These are all significant, distinctive times in your child's life. Later on, when you look back at all your photos, it may be the portrait with the braces that tells you (and your child) the most about who she was and what she was going through. One of the favorite photographs of my daughters shows the younger one with missing front teeth and the older one in braces!

# 6

# INTIMATE
# LANDSCAPES

I n ancient Rome, every patrician home had its
family-guardian statue, *Lar Familiaris,* that
oversaw the welfare and prosperity of the household. It was a cheerful-looking figure in a toga
who kept his benign gaze on the household, often
from his perch in a little cupboard, niche, or freestanding shrine. Members of the family might or
might not take note of his presence as they went
about their daily affairs. But whether or not they
paid attention, the *Lar Familiaris* kept constant
watch over his intimate landscape.

Now, a couple thousand years later, household gods are not quite as popular. But we still
have our intimate landscapes—little areas of
household turf that can remind us of what's most
important to us.

PREVIOUS PAGES Playing with perspective to create a fascinating interior landscape, a collection of colorful ceramic jugs stands against the background of a beautiful landscape mural. RIGHT I found a new use for vintage sterling-silver compacts and cigarette cases when I began using them to display small photos, which I cut to fit and backed with Velcro. Each image case is like a Victorian-era locket holding a portrait of family or loved ones.

In this chapter I want to introduce you to some of the intimate landscapes that people have created in their households—each landscape uniquely suited to the home's interior and the soul of family life. In viewing these homes, I'm sure you'll be reminded of the intimate landscapes that you have already started to preserve as your own, perhaps without even realizing it. And I'll give you some guidelines for creative ways to make these intimate landscapes aesthetically pleasing as well as personally meaningful.

OPPOSITE Sometimes less is more, as exemplified by the simple, clean appearance of this living room. As done here, you can use trays to highlight special objects and treasured collectibles.

## CHOOSE YOUR SITE

An intimate landscape can be located almost anywhere around the home—on tabletops, shelves, mantels, or buffets, wherever there is a flat surface. What makes it "intimate"? It's all in the details.

In my own home, one side table has become a display area for a miniature landscape of engraved silver cigarette cases I've selected or created over the years. Each is filled with miniature photos, and when you open them up, it's a wonderful surprise to find the family photos inside. They come in numerous shapes and sizes, but grouped together, they make quite an impact. Their arrangement is dictated completely by my own personal style. (I could never bring myself to line them up in neat rows—that's totally against my nature!)

# CREATE A
# MULTIDIMENSIONAL
# COLLAGE

If you put your intimate landscape within the "frame" of a tray or table-top, consider all its dimensions. You might begin by thinking of it as a blank, two-dimensional canvas where you can place the pieces in spatial relationships that make sense when viewed from above. But what happens when you look at this landscape from a different angle? You may see possibilities for heirlooms that provide three-dimensional shapes, or add a keepsake that provides an extra accent of form or color. The most interesting landscape, after all, is more than grids and squares. It has hills, valleys, winding channels, and perhaps a mountain or two.

ABOVE This eclectic, multihued assortment of collectibles and treasures shows how texture plays a role in design. Souvenirs from world travel include objects of ceramic, jade, leather, coral, and velvet, artfully combined in a single vignette.

# ARRANGING YOUR FAMILY VIGNETTE

Do you have a collection of framed photographs that you like to keep in your personal space or on a side table? If you're someone who tends to favor neatness and order, you may be tempted to put all your favorite family photos in frames that are identical.

Identical frames are fine for wall-hung photographs, but it's a different story if they're all going on a single flat surface like a shelf or side table. If all the frames are the same height and color, they lose their individuality. Go for different heights. Choose frames that are as distinctively individualistic as the photos inside them.

One of the distinctions I make is between "cold" and "warm" frames. For instance, I would consider silver, black, or glass to be a cold frame. A warm frame could be brass, a brown wood, a vegetable shade of leather, or a soft color.

Consider isolating one photograph all by itself. If it's one of those photos that captures a moment, it doesn't deserve to be in competition with anything else. A photo that makes its own statement, and marks a significant moment in the history of your family, should have a place by itself.

Once you have an arrangement you like, you'll find that the frames become as familiar and companionable as the images they hold. It's like recognizing your best friends by their favorite outfits.

ABOVE Frames come in a wide range of materials and textures, like the ones shown here—made of python skin, alligator leather, silver, and wood.

|| ABOVE Warm colors and vintage brass frames of varying motifs and sizes unify the collection of photos.

# RAISE THE VOLUMES

I love staging books, providing platforms of various heights. When you pile up books, they make a perfect place where you can lean a framed photo or place an inscribed keepsake. By stacking up books to different heights, you actually *create* a landscape. The objects you place on top have a position of prominence, while the pages of your books serve as ideal hideaways for important notes or beautiful bookmarks. In so many ways, books are the ultimate accessory in an intimate landscape. Each has a story to tell—whether truth or fiction. What better way to display a story than with a book that tells another story?

## SOMETHING TO LEAN ON

Not certain where to place a framed photograph? When in doubt, just place it on a shelf or mantel with the top of the frame leaning against the wall. Sometimes you can even lean one frame on top of another, overlapping them, as if they were just placed there for the moment (which they may be). The effect is casual, and invites anyone—family, friends, or guests—to pick up the framed picture for a closer look.

And it's a perfect way to give that image a tryout to see if you like it in your private space. If so, you can find a more permanent place for it on shelving or a wall. But if you just lean it somewhere for a while, it makes that later decision easier.

TOP Securing each photo with picture wire attached to the wall will ensure that the frames won't tumble off accidentally.

ABOVE Place your artwork or photograph on a small easel— it's a wonderful addition to any tabletop and makes the piece seem more special.

# GATHER YOUR MEMORIES
# IN GROUPS AND CLUSTERS

A skilled designer looks for relationships among objects that echo one another in form or color. In a personal collection, you have absolute freedom to play the role of your own designer, any way you want to. Bring together your favorite objects that belong together . . . for any reason. Look around your house. Have you been collecting things over the years that have never been brought together in one place? You may have a collection or a set of memorabilia that's scattered among various rooms of the house, but until you bring them together, you can't really see your collection for what it is. Bring them together in one room, on one table, or on a single tray, and . . . voilà! A collection is born.

ABOVE Consider what can be done with flea-market finds. Placed on a shelf, in juxtaposition to classic views of sailing ships, these vintage bowling pins assume the stature of beautiful sculptural objects.

**TOP** To show off multiple pieces of art, lean them against a large mirror like the one on this mantel. The mirror's frame adds dimension to the modest-sized works, giving them grandeur of scale.

**ABOVE** Among the objects on this mantel are many conversation pieces that the owner collected in his travels or inherited. Adorning the front of the mantel is a nineteenth-century hand-made, beaded lambrequin.

**RIGHT** When you hang anything in front of a mirror, it becomes a highlighted showpiece. In this room, the reflected shadow of a vintage clock makes it look as if it's hovering in another dimension.

## LET YOUR MANTEL TELL A STORY

Traditionally, the hearth was the heart of a home. Even today, the mantel above the fireplace is like a special place of honor. What do you place there? It seems like the ideal spot for an intimate landscape that can be altarlike in its arrangement—with precious glassware or totemic figures. Or it can become a casual resting place for framed photographs that you lean against the wall, side by side with miscellaneous collectibles that make you feel totally at home, surrounded by friends and family even when alone.

Whatever atmosphere you create with the landscape of the mantel is sure to exercise some influence over the entire room, particularly when a blazing fire is lit and the fireplace becomes a source of warmth and a dynamic center of attention. Depending on your tastes, this may be the place for candlesticks, pottery, glassware, shells, found objects, mementos, china, or figurines. And it would be appropriate if each object held special significance, since the hearth is also the place where families have always gathered to hear stories told.

ABOVE Setting the tone for the entire room, the images of sailing ships capture a piece of history related to this shorefront house: for many years it was a boarding school for young yachtsmen.

# BRING OUT
# A COLOR

Just as effectively as historical motifs, color can also be used as a visual link between an intimate landscape and the larger context of a room. In the home designed by Jamie Drake (shown here), a colored-glass collection draws attention to itself in the intimate landscape that Jamie created on a central tray. Jamie's inspiration came when his client, a collector of colored glass, asked him, "How can I display all this?" Jamie used the hue to create a color theme that's picked up and carried through every part of the room, even in the painting.

What's remarkable is the way Jamie—a master at working with color—has made these heirlooms a focal point of the room by echoing their color in the blue walls of the room and in many of the furnishings that surround them. The effect is powerful. At first glance, it may be hard to define why this very large room seems so unified. But the essence of the accomplishment is uncomplicated: just use the power of color to expand an intimate landscape to the outermost horizon of a room's boundaries.

ABOVE The careful placement of white candles against a white background helps accentuate the delicate balance of shapes and forms on this uncluttered mantelpiece.

OPPOSITE The array of color tones in the owners' glass collection influenced their choice of pillows and artwork.

ABOVE A large antique mirror gives the illusion of looking through a window into an intimate private parlor, giving the effect of adding an extra dimension to the room.

OPPOSITE For a setting where people gather in a large room, a serene backdrop is needed. Here, the yellow drapery on one side of the room is offset by the screens opposite, creating a visually peaceful backdrop for intimate accessories placed in the room.

# MAKE THE WALL
# PART OF THE
# LANDSCAPE

I've been intrigued by the ways people have suc-
cessfully integrated intimate landscapes with
larger areas around the home. One of my favorites
(page 149) is a dining room that suggests a lifestyle more than a century old. The family's tastes
run to antiques, and they have inherited many
heirlooms with historical significance, including
furniture, art, pottery, glass, and stoneware. The
comfortable room encapsulates another era—and
within the room there are many intimate land-

scapes, like small tableaux, that have fascinating
attraction.

These smaller settings are integrated into the
larger artistic and historical context of the room.
At one point the family hired a local artist to paint
a mural of the area where the family now lives—
not as it is today, but as it was a hundred years ago.
This was so skillfully done that the mural itself
looks like the work of a nineteenth-century artist,
but closer examination reveals family names integrated into the mural. Ingeniously, without calling
great attention to the correlation between the room
and the painted wall, the room's intimate landscapes have been blended with the background
setting.

**ABOVE AND OPPOSITE** Family names have been hidden in the wall paintings, commissioned by the owner, that portray a history of the local region.

# MEMORIES TO HOLD
# IN YOUR HAND

**Gathered over the span of their lifetimes during long-distance travels that have led from dusty flea markets and high-end auction houses to far-flung continents, each of the items in the home of DeBare Saunders and Ronald Mayne seems to be some part of an intimate landscape.**

"I can remember where everything came from," says DeBare as he picks up a seashell he found decades earlier on the Italian Riviera.

As soon as I came into their house, I noticed many signs of the owners' lifelong passion for collecting. The most casual glance reveals a consuming interest in all things having to do with the beaches and oceans of the world. On shelves, mantels, and tabletops, in glass and china bowls, in every room of the house, seaside vignettes are composed of coral, seashells, and beautifully detailed objects and paintings that reflect a preoccupation with the water.

DeBare recalls idyllic summers in the Hamptons where, as early as he can remember, he began picking up colorful shells that had washed ashore. His steadfast interest in all things aquatic was soon recognized by members of his extended family, and before long his relatives became contributors. An aunt or cousin returning from a seaside trip would bring him shells or souvenirs. When DeBare and his brother traveled to Europe with their parents, he returned with treasured shells from the Mediterranean or the North Sea.

Today, each of these treasures has its place in DeBare and Ron's home. And each item, more precious to the owner than it could possibly be to

OPPOSITE From the filigreed silver salt and pepper servers with tiny crab replicas to the swirling scallop patterns of the dessert plates, this table setting has an unmistakable sea-life motif. The claw-shaped, covered ramekins are for serving lobster soufflé. ABOVE In this glass-topped, velvet-lined case are objects that look like museum pieces, each with a history and meaning connected to the owners' memories, families, and personal associations.

RIGHT A collection of shells within shells; some are rare and precious while others have emotional value because of the memories associated with them.

OPPOSITE In some homes, every item has special meaning. Here, the scallop-backed chair—once owned by the great magician Harry Houdini—is one of the most treasured possessions.

anyone else, serves as a reminder of the place that was visited or the generous person who brought it home. Set on a tabletop is a nineteenth-century Japanese iron crab that DeBare bought when, as a boy, he had only a few dollars to spare. In another room, a sterling silver crab with ruby eyes is poised on a tabletop.

"Backgrounds change, but objects go with you," says DeBare. "If I go away for a long period of time, I take one or two things with me. I don't need to carry photographs because each of these things carries its own picture story with it."

Ron and DeBare's home also contains many intimate landscapes that remind them of important events in their family histories. One carefully arranged display case tells part of the story, with significant objects that speak to them of their heritage. There is the medal that Ron's dad was awarded for his service in the Canadian army during World War II. A star emblem with a crown is the Knight of Malta Award given to DeBare by Queen Juliana of the Netherlands. The memory of Ron's mother is honored with a beautiful gold miniature of Lincoln Center, given to her in recognition of her generous contribution to the building of the Metropolitan Opera House. And from DeBare's

OPPOSITE With the backdrop of silvery silk drapery, the three levels of the bamboo-edged étagère are like miniature stages presenting tableaux of shells and small sculptures. LEFT This sidelong view of a glass-topped table (seen from above on page 151) shows how beautifully it works as an integrated piece of furniture as well as a display case for highly prized objects.

aunt—who, on one visit, caught her nephew sitting in stunned admiration of her rare antique collection—is the ivory monkey that was sent home with him as a special gift.

Memories of Ron and DeBare's shared travel adventures are also contained in this display. Rescued from the Andes are some original pre-Columbian gold pieces. In one of their visits to South America, DeBare discovered that dealers were collecting these ancient artifacts from the indigenous people, then melting them down to resell the gold. Making the acquaintance of the owner of a gold-smelting factory, DeBare rescued the originals before they could be destroyed. They now occupy a prize position—nearby a Murano glass head and an enameled eighteenth-century pill case—in this collection that encapsu-

lates memories of many loved ones and of many travels together.

"If you have more than two or three of something, that's the beginning of a collection," says DeBare. "Once there's an emotional connection, it will continue. Those two or three things could end up being hundreds."

Each object in a collection is part of a living memory. "As you walk through the collection, you walk down memory lane," says DeBare. "It's a wonderfully kaleidoscopic experience, to remember buying it, finding it, or being given it. It's a very visceral emotion."

To me that's the true definition of an intimate landscape—where everything in view reminds you of a personal experience, and you have the satisfaction that comes with a mission accomplished.

# AN IMAGE IN A CASE OR LOCKET

What happens when you open up a silver case or locket and find, inside, a special picture or inscription? Instantly, you feel the connection that must have existed—or still exists—between the person who owns the piece and the cherished image or message that is contained inside.

Sizing a photo to fit inside a locket or case is very simple to do. And because this is a tradition that I would love to bring back, here's how:

» If you have a color or black-and-white photograph, make a copy or take it to a local copy shop and have it reduced. (You don't need to use the original photograph, particularly if it's your only copy or if it's heirloom quality.)

» If you're working with a digital image, the cutting and sizing can all be done on the computer.

» Using the exterior of the case or locket as a template, cut the image to fit.

» For vintage pieces, use double-sided tape or Velcro strips to hold the image inside the case. (For newer pieces, tape or Velcro may not be needed because the images just slide into place in a prepared plastic sleeve.)

ABOVE When I found these vintage cases in flea markets, I was intrigued to discover old messages and engravings left by their earlier owners. Today, these hold photographs of my own family.

OPPOSITE Each one of these image cases, an important keepsake, holds a family photograph that has been photocopied and trimmed to fit inside.

# DEVOTED
# SPACES

A t the beginning of this book, I introduced you to a devoted space—namely, my studio—dedicated to a vocation I'm passionate about. It's obviously one of the favorite places in my home, since photography is so important to me and so much a part of my life. In this chapter, you'll find many other examples of spaces in the home that feel like they're thoroughly taken over and inhabited by a family member, creating a special location set aside to enjoy an all-consuming interest.

In my house there are no barriers between the studio and other living areas. That's true of many devoted spaces shown here. A display like the doll collection on page 170 may fill a whole room. On the other hand, one dedicated area might be as small as a walk-in closet like the one holding a collection of ribbons on page 164. But whatever the location, it's never off-limits. When you're passionate about something, you want to share your enthusiasm—and these areas of the house provide the opportunity to do just that.

# SPECIAL ROOMS FOR CONNOISSEURS

In Rex Stout's Nero Wolfe novels, the impressively cerebral detective is depicted as having a passion for fine dining and exotic orchids. The food preparation he left to his cook, but the orchid room was all his—a perfect example of a devoted space—where his careful and contemplative gardening could not be interrupted unless there was a dire emergency.

While you may not have a greenhouse to devote to indoor gardening, anyone with a green thumb will need a light garden or brightly lit window where you can enjoy, year-round, what you love to do best. But that's only one of the many avocations that require devoted space. Those who love to cook, for instance, will want to arrange and equip their own kitchen "just so," and with reason. This is where you spend many enjoyable hours coming up with the culinary creations that you love to make.

I've seen many other examples of connoisseurs who have succeeded in making over an area so it's expressly their own. If you're a fan of jazz, you'll want your own listening area where you can also keep recordings, posters, and concert

PREVIOUS PAGES An opened drawer displays a beautiful watch collection of both inherited and discovered items, meticulously organized by color and shape. The owner chose the drawer lining fabrics in keeping with the feel of the vintage timepieces.

OPPOSITE Once you have a theme for a collection, you'll soon find many objects that are related. At this entrance to a connoisseur's wine cellar, an intriguing variety of corkscrews (tacked up on corkboards!) is the perfect way to welcome visiting wine enthusiasts.

LEFT In a corner room with floor-to-ceiling windows, the daybed is perfectly placed to create a space where the natural environment seems to literally come indoors.

memorabilia. Theater and movie buffs have similar needs.

One wine connoisseur, for instance, created the beautiful grottolike room shown opposite. The owner keeps his ever-growing (and frequently sampled) collection of wines in a redwood-paneled room with a brick-lined floor. You enter between walls hung with antique corkscrews of all shapes and sizes, from all eras.

The collector of these fine wines first developed an interest when he was in business school. During a summer internship with a consultant who was a connoisseur, he got his first lessons in selection and tasting from his mentor. During that summer, he not only developed a taste for the grape but also a compelling desire to educate himself in all the lore connected with the heritage of wineries and fine vintages.

When this connoisseur and his family moved to their present shorefront home, he created a room totally dedicated to his enthusiasm. Today, when fellow wine lovers pay a visit, he introduces them to this room like a docent to a museum filled with rarities. And, indeed, it is.

## MAKE WAY FOR CHILDREN'S MEMORIES

Upon entering the long upstairs hallway in the house shown here, you'll see immediately how the children's lives and interests are honored with a special place in this household. Even the mirrors are made for kids! Going to and from their bedrooms, they glance up to see their reflections in curved, fun-house mirrors that make their reflections look curvy, skinny, fat, tall, or small. All along the top of the classic chests are many

ABOVE Placing hat forms together turns these old factory items into a collection of art.
OPPOSITE Kids' artwork is prominently displayed in the hallway leading to their bedroom, while funhouse mirrors add a playful touch to the scene.

RIGHT Kids feel more ownership when they see decorative touches that relate to important moments in their lives—like this utilitarian closet space that has been personalized for a young girl by trimming it with her many prize ribbons.

examples of the children's artwork. Farther down the hall are bookcases with shelves beneath that are loaded up with photo albums the kids can take out and explore, interspersed with stuffed animals, puzzle books, and games.

Obviously, adults also come and go along this hallway, but essentially this is a space devoted to the children and their interests. Even the antiques that are displayed—the hat forms and shoe lasts—seem more like toys than heirlooms. And the presence of the children's art is clearly a reminder, to them, of just how important they are in the creation of this family's home.

Some children develop their interests very early—in sports, animals, crafts, games, or collect-

ing. Before long you'll begin to see signs of their special preoccupations, perhaps a shelf dedicated to a model-airplane collection, posters of movie stars or favorite singers, or a pile of autographed programs. But perhaps there's an area in your house, apart from their own bedrooms, that you can "assign" to them as a place to call their own.

Not long ago, I saw the room of a young teenager who was very involved in competitive sports whose parents made a special place for her collection of ribbons and prizes. The walk-in area next to her bedroom (above) was turned into a space dedicated to all her awards. What a great idea! Every time she steps inside, she can remember where she competed and feel a renewed sense of pride.

# THE GAMES
# PEOPLE PLAY

When we speak of a game room, we usually think of a place for kids. But adults have games, too—lots of them—and we deserve our own spaces. For someone who loves to do crossword puzzles, all you need is a comfortable armchair with a magazine rack to hold finished and unfinished puzzles. If your game is pool or billiards, you'll want a whole room where you can shut the door and play undisturbed. For backgammon, mah-jongg, canasta, bridge, or poker, the only space required is a table and four chairs. But real aficionados often have dreams of more. And if you have the resources to realize those dreams, perhaps you will end up with the ultimate game room.

The space shown above and on the following pages is a perfect example of an entire room devoted to one person's passionate interest in the history and the game of chess. Filled with numerous chessboards, timer clocks, and reference books, the room is both a retreat and an entertainment center. The tables are beautifully preserved relics from a chess club that closed down. The timers are souvenirs of championship matches. Here is an ideal retreat for reflecting on tactics, strategy, and history, permeated with reminders of a game in which memory is everything.

ABOVE AND FOLLOWING PAGES Given the patience and the means, you can create an entire domain to hold your prize collection. In this devoted space, the owner has assembled chess tables from the Manhattan Chess Club, one of the oldest in the country, with chess sets that once belonged to world champion Bobby Fisher.

OPPOSITE A testament to the effectiveness of eBay exploration and flea-market searches, all the findings are hung up on the walls to create an impression of a wilderness cabin.
LEFT Patterned cushions and casually draped country blankets are small touches adding to the rustic feel of the environment.

# CREATE AN ATMOSPHERE

Some people love the feeling of literally "stepping into another world," even in their own homes. You really can create that feeling if you know the effect that you want to achieve and collect the furnishings you need to realize your vision. A city apartment can have rooms as rustic as a country cabin or as nautical as an admiral's chart room. In the recreation room of a suburban home, you can conjure the atmosphere of a New Orleans jazz club, a fin de siècle Parisian apartment, or an Empire-era drawing room. All it takes is imagination, some reference materials, and devoted attention to detail.

In the home shown here, all the elements of a single room help to evoke the universe that any outdoorsman would love to inhabit. With its timber siding, stone fireplace, and Adirondack-style furniture, this space is clearly devoted to the interest of someone who loves the idea of outdoor sports. The actual location could be anywhere. What counts most to the creator is the atmosphere, which is as rustic and welcoming as an Adirondack country lodge. This owner has succeeded in creating a cozy cabin environment that you could envision somewhere in the midst of a mountain wilderness.

# LET A COLLECTION REIGN SUPREME

People's collections often have mysterious, but very personal, origins. And once a collection begins, there is no certain or finite end. Ideally, we would have infinite space to hold the things we collect. Since that is never possible, the challenge is to find *some* space we can devote to the ever-growing tribe of collectibles. As for what you keep in that space, your personal passion will be the determining factor. You may need numerous shelves, cabinets, sideboards, and breakfronts to house china, silver, stoneware, or pewter. Or, if you have a collection that's more delicate and miniature in scale, the main requirement is a place that's safe and secure, where neither children nor negligent visitors are likely to cause a catastrophe.

Anyone fond of collecting classic dolls can draw inspiration from the way Mona Pierpaoli has chosen to shelter and display her own collection shown here. Mona's interest in collecting dolls began soon after her daughter was born, and now it's an immensely pleasurable hobby that she shares with her daughter, with members of the Jenny Lind Doll Club (founded in 1938 and still thriving), and with avid collectors from around the world. All of her dolls, including the Japanese ones, are from the late nineteenth and early twentieth centuries. Mona only collects those that were actually played with by children, as opposed to reproduction dolls manufactured exclusively for adults.

The French dolls of that era have heads made of finely manufactured, hand-painted porcelain, and they're dressed in period costumes that reveal the eras in which they were made. The dolls from nineteenth-century Japan have fragile heads expertly created from crushed oyster shells and glue. In many Japanese homes, such dolls are displayed for a short time, once a year, beginning on the third of March, designated as Girls' Day, *Hinamatsuri*.

All the dolls in Mona's collection are kept in turn-of-the-century airtight and dustproof cabinets that were originally showcases in the shops on Oxford Street in London. As she has steadily added to her collection—aided, at times, by her daughter—she has created a space in her home that is like none other anywhere.

RIGHT Natural wood or painted shelving would be too heavy for this collection, but glass has the lightness, neutrality, and airiness that's ideal for vintage dolls with delicate features and ornately detailed costumes.

OPPOSITE A formal showcase can have a whimsical twist, as evidenced by this imposing vintage desk with cubbyholes holding a collection of monkeys and gorillas.

# WHERE DOES
# A COLLECTION BEGIN?

The genesis of a collection could be an inherited heirloom. Or something that you fell in love with—a work of art, a particular kind of craftwork, or the many other examples that you've seen in this book, from doll collections to stoneware. If you live by the sea, perhaps your first collection was seashells or rocks. Whatever the focus of your passion for collecting, it's great fun to do research on what you're collecting, and then begin the physical search online, or travel to antiques markets in various locations. Over time, as your collection grows and you display the objects of your passion, people are likely to take note. Perhaps they'll give you gifts that add to your collection, or report on "sightings" that could lead you in the right direction. Collecting becomes a participatory endeavor you can share with family and friends. And ultimately, the objects in your collection become topics of adventures and stories, and heirlooms for your family.

The inspiration, I'm sure, is different for everyone, but once you're hooked, it's unlikely you'll ever be quite finished with a collection you've begun. Here's what I've learned from my own experiences and from other people who have given me insight into their passion for collecting:

» First of all, *follow* your passion. If you're fascinated by a certain period of history, a particular genre of art, or one kind of collectible object, you might as well give in and indulge yourself. Money doesn't have to be an issue. Some items may cost more, others less, but their nostalgic value cannot always be measured in dollars and cents. Depending on what you choose to collect, the investment can be quite small. What matters most is having a real desire to pursue what interests you. Once started, you'll find there's no turning back.

» Research the history. The more you understand what you're collecting, the more knowledgeable you become about genuine works of good quality. For a collector, this knowledge is essential.

» Research articles. In your quest for knowledge, Google.com is certainly one of the best sources of comprehensive information.

» Put an alert on eBay. Any time your collectible item comes on the market, you'll get a message to keep you up to date on what's out there. Once you do, you can decide whether it's worth pursuing.

» Talk to dealers. They have a wealth of information. A knowledgeable dealer is like a walking encyclopedia on the topic of your collection.

» When you're traveling, stay on the lookout. The perfect addition to your collection might be one town away. Before you go anywhere, be sure to look up shops or markets that specialize in what you're collecting.

» Ask family members about handed-down objects. They may have things in storage that you definitely want to add to your collection.

» Find out who else in the world shares your obsessions. If you happen to be a collector of cookie jars, it may interest you to know that Andy Warhol was an avid cookie-jar collector. In other words, you may have lots of company—and not even know it.

OPPOSITE Use an heirloom to hold heirlooms! This German apothecary case, which originally held all kinds of herbs and medicines, now displays a remarkable, eclectic collection of old cookie jars.

# THINK BEYOND UTILITY

For someone who loves to do pottery, woodworking, or metalwork, a garage or basement workshop is Valhalla. For a horse lover, the best moments of the day are those spent walking and grooming your horses, or working around the stable.

In one sense, these are purely utilitarian locations. But why treat them that way? If you're the craftsperson or the equestrian who relishes the time you spend in your devoted space, why not add more livable areas? The photo above shows how a thoroughly utilitarian stable has been turned into a living area that's as comfortable as a club lounge. This happens to be a stable ruled by a beautiful, temperamental Peruvian named Fantastical and two other horses. The owner is a woman who has been riding since she was a little girl, and one of her daughters has now turned horse-lover as well. Mother and daughter often go riding together. Even without the necessity of exercising the horses or tending to the tack and feed, they're happy to spend every spare minute around the stable. And it has all the furnishings needed to make anyone feel comfortable. Though the occupants are equine as well as human, both share all the comforts of home in this elegant devoted space.

OPPOSITE In a wood-lined stable, the owner took advantage of an empty wall to hang a five-foot-high portrait of her favorite horse, Fantastical.

ABOVE A three-dimensional piece of sculpture, a cherished saddle has pride of place at the tack room entrance, showing off the exquisite handiwork.

# IN A ROOM OF MY OWN

**How do you know when you have a "devoted space" that is really your own? My answer is encapsulated in a quote from the great photographer Henri Cartier-Bresson. "Taking photos," he said, "is to put one's head, one's eye, and one's heart on the same axis." When you walk in, sit down, and spend time in your devoted space, I think that's the way you feel—that your head, eye, and heart are on the same axis.**

I'm fortunate to have such a large area of the house where I can devote myself to my work. But on the other hand, my studio would seem incomplete if it was *just* a workshop and nothing more. What I love is spending time in an environment where I have all the tools I need along with distractions I enjoy equally. Even while single-mindedly concentrated on a project or assignment, I feel wonderfully surrounded by reminders of my family, my photographs, and my personal history.

Among the many cameras that I keep in my studio is one that I never use, but that constantly reminds me of how I started to develop an early love for photography. It's my father's Rolleicord, which had been given to him by *his* father. I understand that he, too, was an avid photographer. My dad used to keep the Rolleicord in his study, but for years it never worked. One year, just before his birthday, I took it to a camera-repair expert in New York City, secretly had it repaired, and presented it to my father on his birthday. He was thrilled.

Near that Rolleicord is my own first camera, the one I used when I was a seventeen-year-old taking a summer-school course in photography in Salzburg. Technically, that first camera of mine has some serious flaws, but even those proved benefi-

cial because they made me work harder and plan more carefully for each shot. It had to be focused the old-fashioned way—by pacing off the distance between camera and subject, then setting the camera for the exact number of feet or meters to create a sharp image. But it was a top-quality Rollei, and it had a Zeis lens, one of the best. Just as there are memories attached to my photographs, the cameras themselves are an inspiration, reminding me of the genesis of my love of photography. So even though I don't use the Rolleicord today, I keep it out where I can see it.

There are many other things in my studio that bring back great memories. I also have a number of white porcelain pieces, a collection that started with a single white mug with the name "Agnes" on it. And therein lies a story. . . .

My grandmother had the name Agnes, and so did my great-aunt—a generous, cheerful, and hard-working woman who made a particular impression on me. Aunt Agnes lived on a farm in Austria that my family visited several summers. It was a real old-fashioned farm with pigs and cows and chickens. We slept in featherbeds double the height of ordinary mattresses that sank down and absorbed you in a mountain of soft warmth. Going to the

PREVIOUS In my studio space I have covered the walls with cork, on which I tack up unframed photos and hang some that have been framed, rearranging them constantly as I add new work.
RIGHT When you begin to explore different combinations of frame and image, you may surprise yourself with what works. I discovered that three photographs of my own daughters fit beautifully into contrasting frames—one new, one vintage, and one hand-engraved.
OPPOSITE My cherished Agnes cup, now dwarfed by larger McCoy and Redwing pieces, was the original inspiration for an ever-growing collection of white porcelain.

outhouse at night meant trekking across the barnyard, past chickens and pigs that made spooky noises. In the afternoons my great-uncle would sit out on the lawn under a pear tree like the baron of his estate, nursing a cognac while he reminisced with neighbors and compeers.

When there was chicken soup to be made, Aunt Agnes took matters into her own hands. At dawn, we would hear the sounds of one disturbed and desperate chicken—a "brawk-brawk-brawk" followed by one prolonged and final "brawwwwwwwk." Somewhere out of sight, a neck was wrung, feathers flew, and for the rest of the day we were treated to the herbaceous aroma that rose from the pot on the stove. Even the consumption of Aunt Agnes's chicken soup was a bit exotic. She stirred the soup with a long-handled wood stirring spoon called a *kochlöffel*, and when she served it up, we ate with spoons that were almost as deep as the *kochlöffel*.

As for how we spent our time, we fed pears to the pigs, ran around with the neighbor kids through the fields while the parents picked potatoes, and at night, settled into our eiderdown cocoons, falling asleep to the discordant sound of crickets.

All that, and more, comes to mind when I glance at the mug on my table that used to belong to my aunt Agnes. But the years have brought about a slow but steady transformation in my attitude to the name itself. Agnes was given to me as a middle name. As a teenager I hated the old-fashioned dowdy flavor of it and tried to keep my middle name a secret. No longer. Instead, I glance at my Agnes mug from time to time, and like some hollow conch shell that contains sea sounds, this mug cups the memory of a wonderful farm and its inhabitants. I can hear my great-aunt's voice, catch the whiff of steam rising from a pot of the most delicious chicken soup ever created, and wish that I could take my own girls back to that time and place, just to know what it was like. And today I willingly

admit that my own middle name is, indeed, Agnes.

Another important area in my studio is the crowded desk, where a chaos of good memories fit right in with the everyday reminders of obligations and assignments. Here I keep heirloom cases and compacts from my collection as well as a tall corkboard stuck all over with personal notes and cards from friends and clients. There's an old photo of me, my girls, and my husband along with some artwork that my daughters created back in nursery school. And I keep some handprints-in-clay that my daughters made when they were kids.

Looking around me, in this room, I feel like everything I need is within reach. This is the place where, for me, head, eye, and heart are truly on the same axis.

# RESOURCES

Throughout this book I've advocated that you visit flea markets and antiques stores where you can discover all kinds of heirlooms and vintage treasures and make them your own. Sometimes, you'll come across the most precious finds in a small shop or an antiques store on a side street well off the beaten track. You can also check local papers for announcements of the local antiques shows in your area.

A big flea market is not only a treasure trove of found goods but also a magnet for knowledgeable dealers who can help you learn more about your family antiques. If you'd like a good starting point, check out the large, popular flea markets that are listed by region below. I've also listed widely known international flea markets to visit if you happen to be traveling to other countries.

## FLEA MARKETS IN THE UNITED STATES

### WEST

AUSTIN COUNTRY FLEA MARKET, AUSTIN, TEXAS
Year-round, Saturday and Sunday,
10 a.m.–6 p.m.
517-928-2795

A PARIS STREET MARKET, LITTLETON, COLORADO
May through October, first Saturday of the month, 8 a.m.–3 p.m.
www.aparisstreetmarket.com

ROSE BOWL FLEA MARKET, PASADENA, CALIFORNIA
Year-round, second Sunday of each month,
9 a.m.–3 p.m.
(early VIP admission available)
www.rgcshows.com
626-577-3101

SAN JOSE FLEA MARKET, SAN JOSE, CALIFORNIA
Year-round, Wednesday, Friday, Saturday, and Sunday, dawn to dusk
www.sjfm.com

TEXAS ANTIQUE WEEKEND
Held in various communities between Houston and Austin, Texas, first weekend in April and first weekend in October. Times vary.
www.antiqueweekend.com

### MIDWEST

KANE COUNTY FLEA MARKET, ST. CHARLES, ILLINOIS
First Saturday and Sunday of each month,
Saturday, 12 p.m.–5 p.m.; Sunday, 7 a.m.–4 p.m.
www.kanecountyfleamarket.com
630-377-2252

RANDOLPH STREET MARKET FESTIVAL, CHICAGO, ILLINOIS
Includes Chicago Antique Market and Indie Designer Market
May through September, weekends
Saturday, 10 a.m.–5 p.m.; Sunday, 10 a.m.–4 p.m.
www.randolphstreetmarket.com
312-666-1200

SCOTT ANTIQUE MARKET, COLUMBUS, OHIO
Ohio Expo Center
Monthly, November through March
Saturday, 9 a.m.–6 p.m.; Sunday, 10 a.m.–4 p.m.
www.scottantiquemarket.com

3RD SUNDAY MARKET, BLOOMINGTON, ILLINOIS
May through October, third Sunday of the
month, 8 a.m.–4 p.m.
www.thirdsundaymarket.com

## NORTHEAST
ANNEX/HELL'S KITCHEN FLEA MARKET,
NEW YORK, NEW YORK
Year-round, Saturday and Sunday, 9 a.m.–6 p.m.
www.hellskitchenfleamarket.com

BRIMFIELD ANTIQUE & COLLECTIBLES SHOW,
BRIMFIELD, MASSACHUSETTS
Three times a year, usually May, July, and
September, second Tuesday of the month
through the following Sunday
Starting times vary
www.brimfieldshow.com

BROWNSTONER'S BROOKLYN FLEA,
BROOKLYN, NEW YORK
April through December, Saturday,
10 a.m.–5 p.m., in Fort Greene
January through March, Sunday, 11 a.m.–6 p.m.,
in Dumbo, Brooklyn
www.brownstoner.com/brooklynflea/

RICE'S SALE AND COUNTRY MARKET,
NEW HOPE, PENNSYLVANIA
Year-round, Tuesday, 7 a.m.–1 p.m., and
March–December, Saturday, 7 a.m.–1 p.m.
www.ricesmarket.com

## SOUTHEAST
DAYTONA FLEA AND FARMER'S MARKET,
DAYTONA, FLORIDA
Year-round, Friday, Saturday, and Sunday,
9 a.m.–5 p.m.
www.daytonafleamarket.com

127 CORRIDOR SALE, FROM UNITY, OHIO, TO
GADSDEN, ALABAMA
Mid-August, various days and times
www.127sale.com
800-327-3945

SCOTT ANTIQUE MARKET, ATLANTA, GEORGIA
Atlanta Expo Center
Second weekend of each month, Friday and
Saturday, 9 a.m.–6 p.m., and Sunday,
10 a.m.–4 p.m.
www.scottantiquemarket.com

# INTERNATIONAL FLEA MARKETS

## CHINA
PANJIAYUAN (DIRT MARKET), BEIJING
Year-round, Saturday and Sunday,
4:30 a.m.–5 p.m.

## ENGLAND
CAMDEN LOCK, LONDON
www.camdenlock.net

CAMDEN PASSAGE, LONDON
Wednesdays and Saturdays
www.camdenpassageislington.co.uk

THE NEW CALEDONIAN MARKET,
BERMONDSEY, LONDON
Fridays, 4 a.m.–2 p.m.

PORTOBELLO ROAD, LONDON
Antique Market, Friday and Saturday,
8 a.m.–6:30 p.m.
General Market, Monday, Tuesday, Wednesday,
Friday, 8 a.m.–6:30 p.m., and Thursday,
8 a.m.–1 p.m.
www.portobelloroad.co.uk

## FRANCE

**CHATOU FOIRE AUX JAMBONS, CHATOU**

Twice annually for ten days, usually March and September. Dates vary. 10 a.m.–7 p.m.
www.sncao-syndicat.com

**ISLE-SUR-LA-SORGUE**

Year-round, Saturday through Monday for antiques markets, Sunday for flea market only
+33(0)4-90-38-04-78

**LA BRADERIE DE LILLE, LILLE**

One weekend in September, annually,
2 p.m.–12 a.m.
www.mairie-lille.fr/fr
+33(0)8-10-09-59-00

**LE MARCHÉ AUX PUCES DE SAINT-OUEN—PORTE DE CLIGNANCOURT**

Saturday, Sunday, and Monday, 8 a.m.–7 p.m.
www.marchesauxpuces.fr

## GERMANY

(Note: Berlin has more than twenty flea markets on weekends.)

**STRASSE DES 17 JUNI, BERLIN**

Year-round, Saturday and Sunday, 11 a.m.–5 p.m.

**CRISTKINDLMARKT (CHRISTMAS MARKET), WESTERN GERMANY, EASTERN FRANCE**

Various town squares opening with the start of Advent season at the end of November and continuing until December 23 or 24, 9 a.m.–9 p.m.

## ISRAEL

**JAFFA FLEA MARKET, TEL AVIV**

Year-round, Sunday through Thursday,
10 a.m.–6 p.m.; Friday, 10 a.m.–2 p.m.
+972-3-527-2691

## ITALY

**PORTA PORTESE FLEA MARKET, ROME**

Every Sunday, 7 a.m.–1 p.m.

## DIGITAL PRINTING WEBSITES

If you've begun to enjoy digital photography, you may already be familiar with the names of some of the websites listed below. They're definitely worth exploring, especially if you have an overabundance of images stored in your camera or personal computer. These websites will help you file, store, and access your own photographs. Most offer services beyond photo printing, allowing you to incorporate personal photographs in cards, books, calendars, gifts, and posters.

**WWW.APPLE.COM/IPHOTO**

Organize photos, create slide shows, enhance editing, do online sharing, make prints, photo books, cards, and calendars

**WWW.KODAKGALLERY.COM**

Prints and posters, photo books, cards, frames, and calendars

**WWW.PICABOO.COM**

Photo books and cards

**WWW.SNAPFISH.COM**

Online photo sharing and storage, prints, photo books, and gifts

**WWW.WINKFLASH.COM**

Canvas prints, photo prints and posters, cards, books, and gifts

## FRAMING SUPPLIES

WWW.LIGHTIMPRESSIONSDIRECT.COM

WWW.PRINTFILE.COM

# DESIGNERS

Kenneth Alpert (page 122)
KA Design Group
595 Madison Avenue, 16th Floor
New York, NY 10022
212-223-0314
www.kennethalpert.com

Eric Cohler (pages 22–23 and 123)
Eric Cohler Design
95 Fifth Avenue, 6th Floor
New York, NY 10003
212-737-8600
www.ericcohler.com

Gary P. Crain (pages 78–79)
Crain & Ventolo Associates, Inc.
215 East 58th Street
New York, NY 10022
212-223-2050
www.crainandventolo.com

Jamie Drake (page 145)
Drake Design Associates
315 East 62nd Street
New York, NY 10021
212-754-3099
www.drakedesignassociates.com

Rita Konig (pages 34–35)

Lisa Monteleone and Marco Bonelli (pages 40–43)
BAMdesign
648 Broadway, 8th Floor
New York, NY 10012
212-219-8075
www.BAMdesign.us

Alex Papachristidis (pages 1, 72–73, 75, 76–77,
104–105, 134, 137, and 138–139)
Alex Papachristidis Interiors
300 East 57th Street, Suite 1C
New York, NY 10022
212-588-1777
www.alexpapachristidis.com

DeBare Saunders and Ronald Mayne (pages 142,
150–151, 152–155, and 158–159)
Stingray Hornsby Interiors LLC
5 The Green
Watertown, CT 06795
860-274-2293

Michael Simon (pages 2 and 31–32)
Michael Simon Interiors, Incorporated
942 Third Avenue, 5th Floor
New York, NY 10022
212-307-7670
www.michaelsimoninc.com

James Alan Smith (pages 78–79)
James Alan Smith, Inc.
Post Office Box 2580
Southampton, NY 11969

Mimi Williams (page 91)
Mimi Williams Interiors
158 Peachtree Circle
Atlanta, GA 30309
404-885-1734 or 404-580-9800
www.mimiwilliamsinteriors.com

# PHOTOGRAPHERS

Erica George Dines (pages 76–77)
Erica George Dines Photography
Atlanta, GA
404-522-9390
www.ericageorgedines.com

Steven Randazzo (all pages except 76–77, 69, 91, and 145)
Steven Randazzo Photography
155 West 68th Street, Suite #622
New York, NY 10023
212-580-7474
strandazzo@gmail.com

Lauren Rubinstein (pages 69 and 91)
Lauren Rubinstein Photography
Atlanta, GA
404-932-2815
www.larphotography.com

Wouter (Holland) Vandertol (page 145)
Represented by: GMA
20 Beekman Place, 10D
New York, NY 10022
212-752-6136
www.gmaimages.com

# ACKNOWLEDGMENTS

I have to first thank Ed Claflin. He spent endless hours listening to my theories and explanations of why and how people need to live with the things they love. Always asking me the right questions to bring out the best, he brilliantly translated my ramblings and philosophies into cohesive text.

I was extremely fortunate to be able to work with the talented photographer Steven Randazzo, who has a great eye and sure instincts. Steve, I know it cannot have been easy to take photos with another photographer looking over your shoulder, but you showed great patience.

Many designers opened their homes to me, or pointed me in the right direction, including Kenneth Alpert, Eric Cohler, Jamie Drake, Rita Konig, Lisa Montoleone, Alex Papachristidis, Gary Crain, James Alan Smith, Michael Simon, Mimi Williams, and DeBare Saunders and Ronald Mayne of Stingray Hornsby.

Thank you to Barkey Powell for all your hard work and management of details—there were so many!

I would like to thank my agent, Stacey Glick of Dystel & Goderich Literary Management, for never giving up on this idea and truly believing in me. We did it, Stacey!

Thanks to my editor, Rosemary Ngo, who, after just having a baby, took on the responsibility of helping to bring another "child" into the world. Many other wonderful people at Clarkson Potter also helped to initiate this project and keep the book on course. I'm very grateful to Judy Pray, my first editor there, for her belief in this project. Thanks to the talented Potter art directors, Marysarah Quinn and Jane Treuhaft, who have been instrumental in making this book beautiful. Thank you, Amy Sly, for such an amazing job with the design of this book. I thank Doris Cooper for also believing in this book and the concept that, yes indeed, people do need to understand that they can live with the things that matter. Thanks to Ashley Phillips, Kate Tyler, and Donna Passannante for all their enthusiasm and hard work.

Of course I have to thank all the wonderful people—clients, designers, artists, and families—who let me share in their personal lives and in turn allowed me to share their lives with you, the readers of this book.

# INDEX

# ABOUT THE AUTHOR

Monica Rich Kosann, nationally recognized fine-art portrait photographer and jewelry and home accessory designer, has secured her reputation as an authority on how people integrate the memories and cherished objects that tell the unique stories of their families into their daily lives. Kosann has been selected as photographer by prominent families in all areas of the arts and business.

Kosann works closely with clients to integrate her candid photographs of children and family into the décor of their homes. She selects from an extensive range of fine-art materials and developing techniques, laying out photographs on walls, reviewing framing options, and creating displays that will be personally meaningful to each family. She encourages clients to frame her photographs as they would any other piece of art, creating what she calls "the fine art of family for the home."

The Manhattan-born daughter of an amateur photographer and gallery owner, Kosann got her first Rollei camera when she was sixteen and started taking art-quality photographs of children when she was seventeen. She studied at the International Center of Photography, Rhode Island School of Design, the Sorbonne in Paris, and the International Academy of Art in Austria. Today, family-photograph assignments take her from her home in New Canaan to clients in New York City, Dallas, Hollywood, Palm Beach, Atlanta, Switzerland, and London.

A number of years ago, Monica and her husband began scouring antiques shows and flea markets for vintage lockets, cigarette cases, and powder compacts that could be adapted to hold family photographs. As demand increased, she developed their own unique line of handmade heirloom-quality, engraved silver display cases, jewelry, and handbags that are now marketed through high-end department stores, boutique jewelry stores, and couture retailers throughout the United States and overseas.

Today, Monica Rich Kosann's brand-name sterling-silver image cases, frames, and jewelry are sold in more than seventy select stores across the country, including Bergdorf Goodman, Barneys, and Neiman Marcus. In 2008, Monica opened her own in-store boutique at Bergdorf Goodman in New York City. The boutique features a charm bar for her Charmed Life Collection, allowing customers to create a custom-made 18-karat gold or sterling-silver charm bracelet.

In 2009, Monica launched www.thefineartoffamily.com, an online magazine and media site that is devoted to stories and videos about how families capture, celebrate, and share their most precious memories. An online boutique for her collection is incorporated into the site.